COLLECTED
ESSAYS OF
Joseph
Murphy

Mentors of New Thought Series

COLLECTED
ESSAYS OF
Joseph
Murphy

DeVorss & Company, Publishers

Second Printing, 1990

ISBN: 0-87516-592-3
Library of Congress Card Catalog No.: 87-70783

DeVorss & Company, Publisher
P.O. Box 550
Marina del Rey, CA 90294

Printed in The United States of America

Contents

These essays were originally
published as separate booklets.

How to Use the Power of Prayer

HOW YOUR MIND HEALS YOU

THERE IS A Healing Presence within you which heals all manner of disease. To use this Healing Presence requires knowledge of God and the way He works.

Spiritual healing refers to wholeness, completeness, and perfection.

Science means knowledge of laws and principles; it means systematized and coordinated knowledge.

Knowledge of this Healing Principle is taken directly from the Bible. The means by which we unlock the mysteries and reveal the hidden meaning of the Bible from Genesis to Revelation is the science of symbology and the science of the Hebrew alphabet.

The Bible deals with spiritual and mental laws. It recognizes the fact that many of the characters, such as Jesus, Moses, Elijah, Paul, and others were real men who lived on earth; nevertheless, they also represent states of mind within all of us. The Bible is a spiritual and psychological textbook.

Through the study and application of mental laws, *you* can find the way to health, harmony, peace, and prosperity; scientific prayer is the practice of the Presence of God.

THREE STEPS IN HEALING

The first step: Think of God as the only Presence and the only Power; God is a universal, creative Spirit present everywhere—the Living Spirit Almighty fixed in your own heart. Dwell on some of the things you know to be true about God; say quietly, for example: "He is Infinite Intelligence, Absolute Goodness, Infinite Power, Indescribable Beauty, Boundless Love, Infinite Wisdom, and All-Powerful.

The second step: Forgive everyone; send loving thoughts to the whole world. Say, "I fully and freely forgive *everyone* now, and I go free." Add sincerely from your heart, "I mean this; it is true." You do not have any mental reservations.

The third step: Claim calmly and lovingly that the Infinite Healing Presence of God within you is now healing your body, making it whole, pure, and perfect. Declare to yourself, "I believe this; I accept it; I know the healing is taking place now." Give thanks for the harmony and peace that are yours.

"God in the midst of you is mighty to heal."

PRACTICE OF THE PRESENCE OF GOD

THE OMNIPRESENCE OF God means that God is present at every moment of time and every point of space. To practice the Presence of God all day long is the key to harmony, health, peace, joy, and a fullness of life. Begin now to see God in every-one and in everything.

THREE STEPS IN PRACTICING THE PRESENCE

The first step: Accept the fact that God is the only Presence and the only Power; He is the very Life and Reality of you.

The second step: Realize the Presence of God in all of the members of your family and in every person you meet. Salute the Divinity from this moment forward in everyone who crosses your path.

The third step: Realize, know, and claim that everything you are and everything you see, whether it is a tree, dog, or cat, is a part of God's expression; this is the greatest thing you can do; it is powerful beyond words.

Sit down quietly two or three times a day, and think along these lines: God is all there is; He is all in all. Begin to realize that the Divine Presence is within you and within everyone around you. *"Seek, and ye shall find. Seek ye first the Kingdom of God, and his righteousness; and all these things shall be added unto you."*

CHANGE FEAR TO FAITH

WHENEVER FEAR enters your mind, it is a signal for ac-tion; do something about it immediately; never surrender to your fear. Your fear is really a desire for something better; it is a longing for freedom and peace of mind. Where will you get your freedom and peace of mind? You will find it in the thoughts of peace, freedom, and poise.

If a man loses his way in the woods at night, fear seizes him; but knowing that God is all-wise and knows the way out, he changes from fear to faith. He is now changing from the mood of fear to the mood of confidence and peace in the only Presence and the only Power. He has changed his mental attitude; this is often referred to as the Angel of God's Presence which leads him out into safety. The man who is lost turns to God in prayer and recognition, and says to himself quietly and lovingly, "God is guiding me now. He is a lamp unto my feet." He trusts and believes in this inner Light; this is the Light that lighteth every man that cometh into the world.

One with God is a majority! There is only fear and love. Fear is love in reverse. Love frees; it gives; it is the Spirit of God. Love builds the body. Love is also an emotional attachment. So fall in love with peace, gentleness, success, goodwill, and harmony, for this form of love casts out fear.

"God is love; and he that dwelleth in love dwelleth in God, and God in him."

THREE STEPS IN BANISHING FEAR

The first step: "The Lord is my light and my salvation; whom shall I fear? The Lord is the strength of my life; of whom shall I be afraid?" *The Lord* means the Presence of God within you. There is no power to challenge God, for God is Almighty. The thing you fear has no power; it is a false belief; it is the bogeyman under the stairs and has no reality. Repeat these wonderful words: "God hath not given us the Spirit of fear; but of power, and of love, and of a sound mind."

The second step: You overcome fear by faith in God and all things good. Faith is not a creed, a dogma, or a religion. Faith is a way of thinking; it is a positive mental attitude. Faith is vital; it is a deep, abiding conviction in God. Faith is the greatest medicine in the world! Take this spiritual medicine of faith now! Look at these words; repeat them: " 'I do all things through Christ which strengtheneth me.' God is with me now. God and His Holy Angels are always with me. I am surrounded by the circle of God's Love." These words are now reflected in your brain and deeper mind. Repeat these powerful statements, and all fear will leave you.

The third step: When fear thoughts come, think of God; imagine you are now resting in the arms of Almighty God in the same way as you rested in your loving mother's arms. Say lovingly to your Father within, "Now, God, I am going about my business, and you are going with me. Your Love, Light, and Power comfort, guide, and bless me in all ways. I love my Father, and my Father loves me; my Father *is* God! It is wonderful!"

OVERCOME WORRY

Worry is due to a lack of faith in God. The person who worries is always expecting things to go wrong. He broods or worries over a great many things that never happen. Such a person tells you all the reasons why something bad should happen, and not one reason why something good should happen. This constant worry debilitates his entire system, resulting in physical and mental disorders.

Your worry can be cured. Do not spend time looking at your troubles or problems; cease all negative thinking. Your mind will not work when it is tense. It relieves the strain to do something soothing and pleasant when you are presented with a problem. You do not fight a problem, but you *can* overcome it.

To release pressure, take a drive; go for a walk; play solitaire; read a favorite chapter of the Bible, such as the eleventh chapter of Hebrews, or 1 Corinthians 13; or turn to the forty-sixth Psalm; read it over carefully and quietly several times. An inner calm will steal over you, and you are ready to pray.

THREE STEPS IN OVERCOMING WORRY

The first step: Every morning when you awaken turn to God in prayer as you would to your loving Father. Relax the body; then talk to God, the only Presence and the only Power. Become as a little child; this means that you realize God is within you; you trust Him completely. *"God in the midst of you is Mighty to heal."*

The second step: You know in your heart that you can present your problems or difficulties to this Power, and that the Wisdom of God will solve them for you. Say lovingly: "Thank you, Father, for this wonderful day. It is God's day; it is filled with joy, peace, happiness, and success for me. I look forward with a happy expectancy to this day. The Wisdom and Understanding of God will govern me during the entire day. God is my partner; everything I do will turn out in a wonderful way. I believe in God; I trust God."

The third step: You are full of confidence and faith. Now let go; and let God work through you. Remember as you go through your day: "This is the day God made for me! There is Divine activity taking place in my life."

DESIRE—THE GIFT OF GOD

GOD SPEAKS to you through desire. All things begin with desire; it is sometimes called the fountain of all action. As you read this, you have within you the urge or desire to be greater than you are. There is a Cosmic urge within you seeking expression. Life seeks to express its unity, wholeness, love, and beauty through you. You are an instrument of the Divine; you are a channel for Life and Love. You are here to release the imprisoned splendor within you.

Without desire you could not move from your chair. Man desires shelter, and he proceeds to build houses to protect himself from the inclemencies of the season. Man plants seeds of corn and wheat in the ground, because he desires food for his family and himself.

You have a supreme desire now; perhaps it is for health, true place, or abundance. Desire unduly prolonged results in frustration and sickness. To desire something good and wonderful over a long period of time, and not attain it, is to waste away in spirit and body. You should learn to realize your desire through prayer; the realization of your desire is your saviour.

THREE STEPS IN REALIZING YOUR DESIRE

The first step: Your desire for harmony, peace, health, true place, wealth, etc., is the voice of God speaking to you. Say from your heart, "With God all things are possible." God is the Living Spirit Almighty within you from which all things flow.

The second step: I am aware of my desire; I know it exists in the Invisible for me. I claim it is mine now; I accept it in my own mind. I have released my desire into the Creative Medium within me, which is the source of all things. I claim and believe that my desire is now impressed in my deeper mind. What is impressed must be expressed; this is the way my mind works.

The third step: I now feel the reality of my fulfilled desire. I am at peace. I know in my heart that what I have accepted as true will come to pass. I rejoice and give thanks. My whole being thrills to the reality of the fulfilled desire. I am at peace. God is peace. Thank you, Father; it is done.

HAPPY MARRIAGE

"WHAT GOD HATH joined together, let no man put asunder." A husband and wife should each be married to God and all things good. A husband and wife should never let the sun go down on their wrath. Never carry over from one day to another accumulated irritations arising from little disagreements. Be sure to forgive each other for any sharpness before you retire at night.

The answer to a happy marriage is for each one to see the Christ in the other; begin *now* to see the Presence of the Living God in each other. Say to yourself now, "I salute the Divinity in my husband" or "in my wife," as the case may be. Say to your wife or husband, "I appreciate all you are doing, and I radiate love and goodwill to you all day long." Do not take your marriage partner for granted; show your appreciation and your love.

Think appreciation and goodwill rather than condemnation, criticism, and nagging. Remember the injunction of the Bible, "Except the Lord build the house, they labor in vain that build it." The way to build a peaceful home and a happy marriage is upon the basis of love, beauty, harmony, mutual respect, faith in God, and in all things good.

Say from your heart, "My marriage is consecrated in prayer and love." A husband and wife should always pray together at least once a day, preferably at night before retiring; this will restore peace in the home and in the heart; for God is peace.

THREE STEPS TO A HAPPY MARRIAGE

The first step: In the beginning, God. The moment you awaken in the morning, claim God is guiding you in all ways. Send out loving thoughts of peace, harmony, and love to your marriage partner, to all members of the family, and to the whole world.

The second step: Say grace at breakfast. Give thanks for the wonderful food, for your abundance, and for *all* of your blessings. Make sure that no problem, worries, or arguments shall enter into the table conversation; the same applies at dinner time.

The third step: Husband and wife should alternate in praying each night. Keep the Bible close at hand. Read the 23rd, 91st, 27th Psalms, the 11th Chapter of Hebrews, the 13th Chapter of 1 Corinthians, and other great texts of the New Testament before going to sleep. Say quietly, "Thank you, Father, for all the blessings of the day. God giveth his beloved sleep."

THE SECRET OF PEACE OF MIND

COMMUNION WITH GOD is the way to peace of mind; this means turning to God in prayer and realizing that His Peace and Love are now flowing through your mind and heart. Prayer, or this silent communion with God within you, will change your character. Prayer makes you a different person.

The word *prayer* may be understood as including any form of communion with God whether vocal or mental. Peace of mind is achieved by getting a real sense of the Presence of God within you. In trying to bring peace into the lives of others, your personal opinion is usually wrong. By interfering in their strife, you usually make matters worse. By getting them to patch up their differences or arriving at a compromise to which they agree, there is no true peace, because they have not completely forgiven each other. The best way to heal quarrels of this nature is the silent way of prayer.

Realize that the Wisdom, Love, and Peace of God are flowing through the minds and hearts of all concerned; the trouble will dissolve in a wonderful way. *"Blessed are the peacemakers; for they shall be called the children of God."*

THREE STEPS TO PEACE OF MIND

The first step: Realize God is Peace, and that He dwells in the midst of you; then think of that inner peace as yours now. Say quietly several times: "The Peace of God that passeth all understanding now floods my mind and heart."

The second step: Know that you have in your mind that which you constantly practice. Say frequently during the day, "I know that peace of mind is mine, because I enthrone thoughts of peace, harmony, and goodwill in my mind; I live with these ideas all day long."

The third step: Read the twenty-third Psalm every night; relax the body; say, "I now enthrone in my mind thoughts of peace, love, and goodwill. God is my shepherd, and God's river of peace flows through me now. I lay me down in peace to sleep; for thou, Lord, only maketh me to dwell in safety."

YOU CAN HAVE A BETTER FUTURE

REMEMBER WHAT JAMES said: "Faith without works is dead." You must demonstrate your faith. Faith is a way of thinking, an attitude of mind, a positive, affirmative approach toward life.

If you live, for example, in the joyous expectancy of the best, invariably the best will come to you. You are demonstrating to the world that your faith is in all things good.

Live in the firm conviction of your oneness with God, with Life, and with the Universe. You will find yourself attracting to you wonderful people, greater prosperity, and increased awareness of God's Wisdom. Claim every day of your life that Divine Intelligence is directing your footsteps along the right path; know that God is your source of supply; He is the giver of every perfect gift. Realize that all of your needs are met, and that there is a Divine surplus.

To attain peace and harmony, say from your heart every morning as you arise, "God's peace, the peace that passeth all understanding, fills my mind and heart." Paul says that all things work together for good to them that love God. God and good are synonymous. You are in tune with all things God-like, and behold, *"If any man be in Christ, he is a new creature."*

THREE STEPS TO A BETTER FUTURE

The first step: In all thy ways acknowledge Him, and He will make plain thy path; trust also in Him, and believe in Him, and He will bring it to pass. Turn to God within you; claim that God is governing all of your affairs.

The second step: Realize that the way to get along with people and adjust yourself to life is to love them. Let your heart be motivated by love and goodwill toward all around you. Pray for the peace and prosperity of all of those with whom you are associated.

The third step: Have a definite mental attitude of success. When presented with a problem, realize that the Infinite Intelligence of God is revealing to you the perfect plan and showing you the way you should go. As you go to sleep say, "God knows the answer." *Feel* the joy of the answered prayer.

OVERCOME IRRITATION

"He whose spirit is without restraint, is like a city that is broken down and without walls." "He that ruleth his spirit is greater than he that taketh a city."

In order that you might lead a full and happy life, control of the emotions is essential. To govern and control your emotions and temper tantrums, it is essential to maintain control over your thoughts. As a matter of fact, you cannot find peace any other way. Willpower or mental coercion will not do it. Forcing yourself to suppress your anger is not the way.

The answer is to enthrone God-like thoughts in your mind; busy yourself mentally with the concepts of peace, harmony, and goodwill. Keep firm control over your thoughts. Learn to substitute love for fear, and peace for discord.

You can direct your thoughts along harmonious lines. For example, if you see or hear of something that disturbs or angers you, instead of giving way to anger or irritation, say automatically, "The peace of God that passeth all understanding is now flooding my mind, my body, and my whole being." Repeat this phrase several times during the period of stress; you will find that all tension and anger disappear.

Fill your mind with Love, and the negative thoughts cannot enter. When someone says something sharp or critical to you, think on a single statement of Truth, such as, "God is Love. He leadeth me beside the still waters." Peace steals over you; you will radiate this peace.

THREE STEPS IN OVERCOMING IRRITATION

The first step: As you awaken in the morning, say to yourself: "This is God's day; it is a new day for me, a new beginning. The restoring, healing, soothing, loving power of God is flowing through me, bringing peace to my mind and body now and forevermore."

The second step: Should some business problem or some person upset or irritate you, think immediately about His Holy Presence. Say, "God is with me all day. His peace, His Guidance, and His Love enable me to meet all problems calmly and peacefully."

The third step: Radiate Love to all of your associates. Claim that they are doing their best. Say, "I wish them peace, harmony, and joy. I salute the God in them." And lo and behold, God and His Love come forth!

YOUR SPIRITUAL REBIRTH

WHEN THE STORM of life disturbs you, and it appears that your ship is about to founder, remember that it is time for you to awaken to the Christ within. This is how you become reborn spiritually: Recall to mind that God is within you, the very life of you. "Closer is He than breathing, nearer is He than hands and feet." Realize that "With God all things are possible." Claim and know that the God-Power within you is able to cope with any difficulty. Dwell on the peace and harmony of God where the difficulty is, and a perfect, Divine solution will follow.

If troubled, say, "Peace, be still!" The peace of God will steal over you. Turn your burdens (your problems) over to the God-Wisdom within you, knowing and believing that the perfect solution will come to you in God's own way. When you do this with faith and confidence, the storm or anxiety will pass away, and a great calm will steal over you; this is the peace that passeth all understanding. If you are living in limitation and sickness, this is bondage and restriction; it means you are in the dark as to the higher side of life and your tremendous potentialities. When you catch a glimpse of a higher set of facts, the old way of thinking will be displaced; then your Christ or inner Life will rise from the dead, or limited state.

Enthrone the concepts of peace, harmony, and success in your mind; busy your mind with these things; you will find that your body and circumstances will reflect your inner, mental attitude; this is the new birth of freedom. Remove prejudices, deceit, and jealousies from your mind by opening your mind to the Light of God's Love and inspiration. God's Love revivifies and thrills you; this is the birth of God in you.

THREE STEPS TO YOUR SPIRITUAL REBIRTH

The first step: "I saw a new heaven and a new earth." I know now that God's Love springs in my soul. My heart feels the Presence of God, because I radiate Love and joy to all.

The second step: Any time a negative, fearful, critical thought comes to me, I say, "God is with me." This kills it; then my soul is filled with Love toward all.

The third step: Remember always that God never changes. God is within you—your loving Father—saying, "Fear not, child, for all is thine!"

Love Is Freedom

The Pharisees also came unto him, tempting him, and saying unto him, Is it lawful for a man to put away his wife for every cause? And he answered and said unto them, Have ye not read, that he which made them at the beginning made them male and female, and said, For this cause shall a man leave father and mother, and shall cleave to his wife: and they twain shall be one flesh? Wherefore they are no more twain, but one flesh. What therefore God hath joined together, let no man put asunder. . . . Whoever shall put away his wife, except it be for fornication, and shall marry another, committeth adultery: and whoso marrieth her which is put away doth commit adultery.
—Matthew 19:3–6, 9

LET US SEE these great truths in a new light. God is love, and when true love in the heart unites a man and a woman together, that is actually God joining a couple in a sacred covenant. When there is a true, spiritual union between two people (*God hath joined*), there is no divorce, for none is wanted. They blend spiritually, mentally, and physically.

16

There is no institution on earth so sacred as that of the home you are about to make and no vows so wonderful as those you make in the marriage ceremony. True marriage is the holiest of all earthly institutions. It should be entered into reverently, thoughtfully, and with a deep understanding of its spiritual significance. Marriage is an accord of Divine ideas, a harmony and purity of purpose. Harmony, honesty, love, and integrity must prevail in the minds and hearts of both husband and wife. From this inner state of conscious unity in these essential characteristics of a successful marriage there comes the outer state which corresponds to it, making the outer like the inner—peaceful, joyous, and harmonious.

When a man marries a woman because of her wealth, social standing, and political connections, or merely because she is young and beautiful and he wishes to exalt his ego, this is not a real marriage. Actually, it is a sham and a farce. When a woman marries a man because of his profession or for her own personal security or for any reason other than real love, such a marriage is false and a masquerade; it is not made in heaven, meaning harmony and Divine understanding.

I have performed marriage ceremonies for men and women of advanced years, sometimes blessed with as many as seventy-five to eighty years, chronologically speaking. The fires of sex have died out in many of these cases; nevertheless, God (love) joins them together for the simple reason that they are honest, just, sincere, and truthful with each other, and they seek a loving companionship where they desire to share their joys and experiences together. Honesty, sincerity, integrity, and justice are children of love, and when these are absent in the marriage ceremony, regardless of age, it is not a true marriage.

A minister, rabbi, or priest officiating at the ceremony does not validate or sanctify a marriage. He merely confirms objectively what the man and woman already felt to be true subjec-

tively, which was a union of two souls seeking their way back
to the heart of God.

How often is marriage a real spiritual union where the par-
ties to the contract blend themselves spiritually, mentally, and
physically? And, on the other hand, how often is it a legal
ceremony against which the husband and wife begin to chafe in
a few weeks? Remember that like attracts like, and if you want
to attract the right companion, use the proven spiritual approach
as follows: Still your mind, think clearly and with interest on
the qualities and attributes you admire in a man or woman, and
mentally dwell on the characteristics that you would admire in
the other, such as whether he or she is spiritual, loyal, faithful,
honest, talented, happy, and prosperous. Gradually these qualities will sink into your subconscious mind. Infinite intelligence
always takes over when you pray this way, and, as a result, you
will irresistibly attract to you the right companion. The man or
woman whom you attract will be the image and likeness of the
ideal on which you meditated. You will harmonize perfectly,
and there will be mutual love, freedom, and respect; this is
called the ''marriage made in heaven,'' or ''peace and understanding.''

The question frequently arises, ''Should I get a divorce?''
This is an individual problem. It cannot be generalized. In some
cases, divorce is not the solution any more than marriage is the
solution for a lonely man. Divorce may be right for one person
and wrong for another. A divorced woman may be far more noble and God-like than many of her sisters who are living a lie
rather than facing the truth. The usual excuses and alibis used
to cover up are that it would be bad for John's business, or the
neighbors would talk, or it would be bad politics, etc. This, of
course, is making a mockery of marriage.

Some time ago I talked with a woman who had been de-
ceived and tricked by her husband. He had told her prior to marriage that he was a representative for an eastern concern, that

he was single, and that he belonged to her church organization—
all lies. It turned out that he was an ex-convict, a wife-beater,
and that he was living with another woman when he married
her. She had advanced him some money, thereby whetting his
taste for more, which is the real reason why he married her. She
thought it was a sin, however, to get a divorce; yet she longed
for freedom and peace of mind. I explained to her that she was
not really married at all, that such a marriage was simply a sham
and a mockery, and that she was living a lie. She thereupon
proceeded immediately to get a divorce and dissolved this
fraudulent marriage forthwith.

I recall the case, during the war, of a young girl who got
highly intoxicated one evening, which resulted in a complete
blackout, and she found herself with a marriage certificate the
next morning. She had married a native of one of the islands.
She was shocked beyond words and had to get psychiatric treatment. She immediately dissolved the marriage.

A great number of people are confused and suffer from a guilt
complex based on misinterpretation of the biblical quotation,
*Whosoever shall put away his wife, except it be for fornication,
and shall marry another, committeth adultery: and whoso marrieth her which is put away doth commit adultery* (Matthew
19:9). The Bible also says: *Whosoever looketh on a woman to
lust after her hath committed adultery with her already in his
heart* (Matthew 5:28).

Here we are told that adultery is of the heart or the mind.
The heart is the seat of the emotions, the feeling nature, the
subjective mind. Acts of the body are determined by the movement of the mind. A hundred years ago, Phineas Parkhurst
Quimby pointed out that the body moves as it is moved upon
by our mind, and the body acts as it is acted upon.

Fornication in Bible language means giving allegiance and
attention to false gods rather than to the one true God—the Living Spirit Almighty within man, which is the supreme and

sovereign Power. The Bible is a psychological document; it points out that when man visits the slums in his own mind and keeps company with mental murderers, such as hate, resentment, anger, or ill-will, he is cohabiting with evil and is therefore guilty of fornication and adultery. In biblical language, he is already divorced for the simple reason that he has separated himself from God for his immediate pleasure. He is cohabiting with evil in his mind, and he is no longer married to peace, harmony, love, and understanding.

Man is fornicating when he mentally and emotionally unites with erroneous concepts, indulges in resentment and anger, or becomes morose and morbid. Whenever men and women are mentally divorced from their marriage vows, eventually there will be a separation or divorce on the external plane. The subjective side of life always controls the objective phase of life.

We must remember that just because a man and a woman have a marriage certificate and live in a home, it does not follow necessarily that it is a real home. Perhaps it is a place of discord and hate. When, for example, a child is present and the parents do not know the laws of life, it is better to break up such a union than to have the mood of hate impair the growing mind of the child. Many times a child's life and mind are dwarfed by the mood of the parents, which in the passage of years often results in neurosis and crime. It is far better for a boy to live with one parent who loves him than to live with two who hate each other and who fight all the time.

Many men and women have told me that they feel very guilty because of what they term "sex sins." They feel that God hasn't forgiven them. I explain to them that God is the Life Principle, that Life does not condemn or punish, and that they are simply condemning themselves and suffering accordingly and needlessly.

God is the Life Principle. If you burn your finger, you know very well that the Life Principle forgives you by reducing the edema and by giving you new tissue. Life has no grudge against you for having burned yourself; It forms a blood clot, builds a bridge of new cells, and forms new skin. If you have eaten some bad food, Life forgives you by causing you to regurgitate, thereby cleansing your system of possible food poisoning. Life always seeks to preserve you. This is the meaning of "God does not condemn or punish you." We punish ourselves by the misuse of our subconscious mind.

Jesus said to the woman caught in adultery: *Woman, where are those thine accusers? Hath no man condemned thee? She said, No man, Lord. And Jesus said unto her, Neither do I condemn thee: go, and sin no more* (John 8:10–11).

The harlot, or the woman with the illegitimate child, who may be condemned and stoned (ostracized) by the world, may turn to the God Presence within and claim her freedom and peace of mind. She realizes that God condemns no one. *Thou art of purer eyes than to behold evil, and canst not look on iniquity* (Habakkuk 1:13). Society and the world may condemn her, or she may engage in self-accusation and self-criticism. *For the Father judgeth no man, but hath committed all judgment unto the Son* (John 5:22).

The *Son* is your mind. This is the place wherein you pronounce judgment on yourself by the thoughts you entertain. God, the Absolute, knows nothing about our errors and fears. You forgive yourself by giving yourself the mood of peace, love, and harmony for the mood of guilt, despair, and self-condemnation.

Turn from the past and completely detach yourself from the former way of living. Mentally and emotionally unite with your aim, which is peace, dignity, happiness, and freedom. As you do, God and His glory responds at once. You will find a wave of peace moving over the arid areas of your mind like the dew of heaven, and the shadows of fear and guilt will pass away. As you cease to condemn yourself, you will find that neither can the world condemn you.

There is nothing evil in sex or in anything else created and ordained by God. *Male and female created he them* (Genesis 1:27). *Therefore shall a man leave his father and his mother, and shall cleave unto his wife: and they shall be one flesh* (Genesis 2:24). In marriage you give yourself completely—spiritually, mentally, and physically. The sex act between husband and wife should be a love act, and each should realize that love is of God and that any children born will be born of that love. The sex instinct is not opposed to spiritual impulses. The sex drive must be channeled constructively, harmoniously, and lovingly. Lust as such is not love; the normal sexual act between marriage partners, however, involves the genuine emotion of love, which is the essence of conjugal love.

Many married men and women have a false, negative attitude toward sex. Some think that it is evil, nasty, and ugly, possibly due to their upbringing or due to some sexual shock in childhood. Often, this attitude results in impotence in men and frigidity in women.

I have had women say to me that their husbands were materialistic and carnal, and that they looked down on their husbands, claiming that they were superior because they despised and hated the sex act. This is pure rationalization and indicates subconscious poison pockets regarding sex, in all probability due to early training and false interpretation of the Scriptures.

A distant relative of mine once told me that before the sex act, she and her husband prayed. There is nothing wrong with prayer, but the reason for their prayer at that time was due to the fact that she looked upon the sexual act as sinful and unclean, and she thought she would exorcise through prayer any evil connected with the act. Basically, she had contempt for sex and was frigid. She said, ''I love my husband spiritually, not physically.'' She separated sexual love from spiritual love.

I explained to her that marriage is a total union of body and soul. *A man . . . shall cleave unto his wife: and they shall be one flesh* (Genesis 2:24). She thereafter began to affirm, "I love my husband spiritually, mentally, emotionally, and physically. He is God's man, and I radiate love, peace, and goodwill to him. God's love flows from me to him, and our sex relationship is joyous, loving, and harmonious. Between us are mutual love, freedom, and respect."

After a few weeks, her frigidity was dissolved, and there was a harmonious marriage. She intuitively perceived a great truth: God had placed in her heart a desire to attract a man, and He had placed in the man a desire to attract a woman.

A few days ago, I talked to a woman who was about to get her eighth divorce. She was exceedingly bitter and resentful toward her present husband as well as toward all the previous ones. She had remarried each time without forgiving and mentally releasing her husbands, and each one was worse than the preceding one. Her inner mood of resentment had caused her to attract similar types of men, based on the law of attraction. The cure was to forgive herself and all her former husbands and to build into her mentality the mental equivalent of the kind of man she desired.

If you strike a key on a grand piano, all the tones in harmony with it will respond. They may be higher or lower, but they are similar. So too do you attract to yourself those people who have qualities based on your mood and concept of yourself. It is affinity or attraction, depending upon the chord you strike. You may strike a discord, but you do not take out all the discords in order to make a harmony. When you discipline your mind in prayer and enter into the spirit of forgiveness, you can play a divine melody.

Suppose that a man cheats on his wife. If he had love and respect for his wife, he would not want any other woman. When a man has found his true, spiritual ideal in marriage, he has no desire for any other woman. Love is a oneness; it is not a duality or a multiplicity. A man who runs around with many women—which indicates the many adulterous moods within him—is marrying many concepts, such as frustration, resentment, cynicism, etc. When you have found love with your mate, you also have found a fullness of life.

You may ask, "Why did some men previously have many wives?" The reason was that at one time the earth was underpopulated, and the earthly fathers, not knowing anything better, followed this polygamous method. Today, we are more spiritually awakened, and we know that the earth is populated enough.

The philanderer has a profound inferiority complex and feels insecure, and all the women he meets are vacillating, neurotic, and confused like himself. He is seeing and hearing his own inner vibrations. "Birds of a feather flock together." "Like begets like."

Let us take the case of the woman who is running around with a married man. Such a woman has been unable to demonstrate a husband or a boyfriend; she gets a pseudo-satisfaction, or false thrill, in stealing another woman's husband. She, too, has an inferiority complex and is unstable.

Man demotes himself by his feeling of lack and limitation. His fear is transmitted to his wife, and she reacts in kind. She cannot see him in the way she formerly did, as he has not the same feeling about himself. She can see him only in the way he sees himself; likewise, he can see her only in the way she sees herself.

If a man feels himself to be dignified, he commands respect and he gets it. A man who has the predominant mood of success and happiness knits together all the members of his household. He is a cementing influence, and there is harmony and peace in his household.

The sex life prevails in the vegetable, animal, and human life. Basically, it is the life force seeking expression in all its varied forms. The sex urge is operating in you through your talents, abilities, feelings, and urges. Whenever you meditate on the truths of God, or upon any idea, and enter into the feeling of it, that also is a phase of sex. Your hunger and thirst for truth, your spiritual awareness and understanding, and your intense desire to reproduce more and more of the goodness of God in the land of the living—these are all spiritual outlets for the sex urge or life force within you.

When you are not fully expressed along all lines and when you do not constructively channel your libido or life force, the emotions become dammed up and bottled up, resulting in frustration, neurosis, imbalance, mental disorders, and in forms of escape in alcoholism and drug addiction.

A man once boasted to me that he had not had relations with his wife for over four years, and he added that he had become more *spiritual*. He belonged to a strange cult, the leader of which had told him that in order to advance spiritually, he had to lead an ascetic life and refrain from all intercourse with his wife. This man was neurotic, afflicted with ulcers, and mentally disturbed. He had been brainwashed into believing that sex was evil and would inhibit his spiritual illumination. I explained to him that all this was pure balderdash and primitive thinking based on ignorance, superstition, and fear of sex.

At my suggestion he renewed normal relations with his wife, looking upon the act as right. He realized that he was God-placed in this world to enjoy all of his senses and to go forth and multiply and replenish the earth. Wise use of our faculties, urges, and desires in moderation in all things is the answer—not repression or suppression. Thereafter his constant prayer was: "We have a happy, joyous marriage, satisfying and harmonious, of true and lasting love. Divine love reigns supreme in our marriage now." Their marriage has been much happier than ever before.

If love is lacking in your life, use this prayer frequently: "God's love, wisdom, and harmony are being expressed through me now. Poise, balance, and equilibrium reign supreme in my life." As you make a habit of this prayer, wonders will happen in your life. Love, inspiration, and guidance will well up spontaneously, and you will become an irresistible magnet attracting to you all the blessings of life from all directions.

Young men and women often ask me if they should experiment before marriage. I tell them that marriage does not change anything and that if they freely indulge before marriage, how can they expect fidelity or trust after marriage?

A young man who was studying physics in New York went in for free love. "Morals," he said, "are a joke." He had no standards, and he was having sexual relations with several girls who attended the same college. One girl became pregnant. Then there followed legal action and a "shotgun" wedding. He had to quit college in order to take care of his wife: he worked as a waiter. He had married a girl he didn't want, and a baby was born that neither of them wanted. Where are his freedom and his free love? He has placed himself in the prison of want, lack, resentment, and poverty.

You are aware that you must curb your appetite for alcohol, fats, ice cream, and cigarettes. Likewise, you must curb your emotions, urges, and drives, and you must see that they are expressed harmoniously and wisely. Your sex life must be blended with love and understanding.

Premarital sexual experiences are not conducive to a happy married life. Often, the man distrusts the woman he can have so easily. He says to himself, "If she will do this before marriage, she will do it with others afterwards." I ask a young man, "Is your girlfriend nobler, grander, sweeter, more dignified in your eyes now than before sex relations?" Usually, he blushes and says, "No, I guess you're right."

Happiness in marriage depends on love, loyalty, honesty, devotion to the truth, integrity, and a desire to lift up each other spiritually, mentally, and in all ways. Love does not take a woman to a shabby motel; neither is real love experienced furtively by an illicit interlude in such a cheap motel.

To maintain a happy married life, pray together and you will stay together. Affirm frequently: "Divine love, harmony, peace, and perfect understanding are now operating and expressed in our heavenly marriage. Morning, noon, and night we salute the Divinity in each other, and all our ways are ways of pleasantness and all our paths are peace."

Mental Poisons
and Their
Antidotes

RIGHT MENTAL ATTITUDE INDUCES HEALING

THERE ARE MENTAL as well as physical poisons. Mental poisons are wrong thoughts which work underground in consciousness like a contaminated stream to emerge even after years in wrong experiences (illness, loss, unhappiness, etc.).

I read some time ago of a scientific experiment in Russia in which six hypnotized and conditioned cats were given cyanide of potassium with no fatal effects, while six other unconditioned animals all died. If we had enough faith in the subjective power of God within ourselves, we could nullify all deadly poisons, mental and otherwise.

What is the prophylaxis? The first step is not to be afraid of the cancer, tuberculosis, arthritis, or mental disorder from this moment. The second step is to realize that the condition is the product of false thinking and will have no more power to continue its existence; then you are exalting the God in the midst of you. This will stop all toxicity in you or the person for whom you are praying.

Pronounce the condition "false" and exalt God by seeing the perfect solution, the beauty, and wholeness made manifest where the trouble is.

Among the most deadly mental poisons are the following: Fear, hatred, self pity, resentment, envy, vengeance, loneliness, and melancholy. All these are modifications of fear. The biblical name for fear is a blind, false thought called Goliath. The word *Goliath* means an aggressive, domineering thought or idea that brags about its power, intimidates, bullies, browbeats, and frightens you into submission to its unrighteous reign. Perhaps you are afraid to meet this gangster, intruder, or marauder in your mind. Maybe you are afraid of results, and you hesitate to meet this sinister shadow openly and rout him out.

It is necessary to play the role of David in order to get rid of this ganster called fear. *David* means a man who loves God, who knows there is only One Sovereign Power which moves as a Unity and knows no divisions or quarrels, and whose name is Love. David, which is your awareness of the Presence and Power of God, killed the Philistine giant called Goliath, or fear, with a stone thrown from his shepherd's sling. Fear is a shadow of the mind held by ignorance and darkness. When you hold your fear to the light of reason and intelligence, it can't stand the light and it disappears. Among the offspring of fear are the following:

(a) *Hatred*, which is really inverted or misdirected love based on ignorance.

(b) *Self-pity*, which is really self-absorption. This mental poison creeps through the psychic bloodstream poisoning the springs of hope and faith, leading to dementia praecox, melancholia, etc. The antidote is to find your *other* self (God) and become intoxicated by realizing your love of God, and your sense of union with the One Power will bring about a new birth of peace, health, confidence, and strength.

(c) *Old-age fear* is another mental poison. Old age is not the flight of years, but the dawn of wisdom, truth, and beauty.

(d) *Loneliness* is a lack of love. The loveless seek love, but the loving find love and friendship everywhere. The antidote is to fall in love with God's companions in your mind. Their names are goodwill, kindness, gentleness, peace, patience, understanding, and a sincere interest in others. Pour out God's Love—a double portion of the Spirit—on those around you; then you will banish loneliness immediately. God will give you a double reward also, and your good will be multiplied exceedingly.

Your state of mind is your master. It is foolish to let that ignorant, blind, stupid monster fear push you around and direct your activities. Consider yourself too smart, too brilliant, for that to happen. Why not become David? Play the role; it will pay you fabulous dividends. David means your faith in God is greater than fear. Fear is faith upside down. Fear is a conglomeration of dark and sinister shadows in the mind. In short, fear is faith in the wrong thing. Become a spiritual giant, call David forth (which is confidence in God). He is within you; summon him. At the same time you can call forth God's Love.

The children of faith in God are love, peace, gentleness, goodness, kindness, joy, balance, tranquillity, and serenity. When you realize that there is but One Power, One Cause—the Maker—you give all your allegiance, devotion, and loyalty to that One; then you become David, beloved of God. David (spiritual awareness) had no armor or material protection such as they used in those days. His power was his trust in the God of his fathers, knowing that Infinite Intelligence knew only the answer to any problem.

When you claim God's guidance and God's direction, you will always see the weak spots in the armor of Goliath or the person who threatens you with dire disaster. Actually it is never the person who has the power, but the thought in your own mind. The enemies are of thine own household (mind). *And David put his hand in his bag, and took thence a stone, and slang it, and smote the Philistine in his forehead, that the stone sunk into his forehead; and he fell upon his face to the earth* (1 Samuel 17:49). The stone is your conviction of the One God, the One Power. A stone is hard and impervious, which means that your faith or confidence in the Spiritual Power is unyielding and inflexible. In other words you are unmoved, undisturbed, unyielding in your attitude, and you trust in the One, the Beautiful, and the Good. With this stone or mental conviction you shatter the forehead of the giant called fear or Goliath. Fear is prone to brag, and in that lies its weakness. David (love of Truth) went forth with one idea: to prove the supremacy of the God-Power. When you go forth in the assurance that "one with God is a majority," you will find yourself guided in every way and you will become the inevitable victor.

Don't fight fear with fear, instead meet it with a direct declaration of God's Presence and Power, which renders fear powerless. Say to yourself, "The Lord is my light and my salvation; whom shall I fear? The Lord is the strength of my life; of whom shall I be afraid?" (Psalm 27:1, 2). Are you afraid of some disease which has gripped you? You will notice that an erroneous thought in your mind can brag and boast of its pseudo-strength and it intimidates you. Don't let these thoughts bully and browbeat you. Meet and subdue them now. Realize that all discord is manufactured by your own mind; it is not something you catch on the outside. You can change your mind by realizing that the Infinite Healing Presence which made your body is healing it now. As you do this consciously and knowingly, there will be a rearrangement of the thought-patterns in your subconscious, and a healing will follow. Your present mental conviction determines your future and your experience.

Meditate and pray upon positive and spiritual values. Claim your ideal, solution, health, or peace of mind upon the basis that the Spirit within you is Supreme and Omnipotent, and by thinking of your solution or ideal with confidence and faith, you are conditioning your mind to the answer. Your mind is full of confidence or fear according to what you put into it. Become David, the ruddy-faced shepherd boy, by partaking of and appropriating your Divinity now. Get the insight to persevere and know that you will meet on life's journey only those experiences which you consciously and unconsciously send before you. Claim that God and His Love go before you; this means the mood of confidence, faith, and trust in an Almighty Power which never faileth. As you do this, you are David going forth in might and right, clothed with the whole armor of God, preparing for yourself freedom, peace of mind, and happiness.

The story in Samuel tells us that David cut the head off Goliath. This is what the spiritually minded man must do with all error, false belief, and superstitions in his mind; he must cremate, burn up, and consume all negative thoughts with the fire of Divine Love and right thinking. Goliath or fear is faith in a false god. You are David properly equipped when you realize you have faith in the One True God—the only Power and Presence.

Recently I was talking to a husband and wife who were convinced that they would lose everything in a lawsuit which had dragged on for five years. They were very pessimistic; it seemed the other side were lying and were, as the saying goes, trying to get something for nothing. Their lawyer told them that in his opinion they didn't stand a chance, and they were hypnotized by that suggestion. I explained to them that the statement or suggestion of the lawyer had no power and that his words could not bring to pass what he suggested. They realized that the only power the suggestion of their attorney had was their mental acceptance of it. They had accepted the suggestion and had reacted accordingly, but the whole process took place in their own minds. They permitted their attorney to suggest the loss of the case to them. All the time the power was in their own thought. They prayed as follows: "God is Absolute Harmony and Absolute Justice; therefore the result is justice, harmony, and satisfaction to everybody." This was their simple prayer. Their premise was true; therefore the conclusion had to be true. Moreover, the beginning and the end were the same. If a man begins with God he ends with God, or the Good. The fruit is in the seed, the oak is in the acorn. There was a perfect, harmonious solution to the lawsuit and it was settled out of court.

God is never late; the secret is in remaining loyal and faithful to that which you know to be true of God. Do not hesitate to draw the sword of Truth like David. Become armed with spiritual reasoning and understanding of Divine Law and the Eternal Verities. Slay ruthlessly and without pity all negative thought-patterns in your mind; order them out in a dynamic, forceful way, and let in the Light, Love, and Truth of God. Your spiritual awareness acts as a sword in that it severs you completely from the old way of thinking, race belief, other powers, malefic entities, and suppositional opposites to the One Supreme, Loving Power.

A woman said to me last week, "I am so mad, I could kill May!" It seems May had spread lies about her and had also tried to undermine her in the position she held. The woman permitted May to disturb her; in other words, she gave power to May which May did not possess. The trouble was in her own thought-life. May was not responsible for the way she was thinking about her; she realized suddenly that the whole trouble was in her own mental imagery and thought-patterns. She let Goliath (fear) run riot in her own mind, browbeating, intimidating, bullying, and frightening her—the whole process being one of her own creation. The young lady had good common sense and she began to vent her spleen on the bacteria of fear, hatred, and resentment in her mind, casting out these mental poisons and neutralizing the toxic effects with right thinking and right feeling. She placed God back on the throne of her mind, saying to herself, "I will fear no evil: for thou art with me" (Psalm 23:4).

Where God is there can be no evil, and as she saturated her mind with the simple truth, "God is; His Presence fills my soul and rules my life," all the ill-will vanished away. She positively refused to let some other woman give her migraine, indigestion, insomnia, and the jitters. No one has that power. The power is in your own thought-life. You are the one to determine how your thought moves. Good and evil are the movements of our own mind. Do not permit thieves of fear, resentment, and inadequacy to restrict, bind, and hold you in the chains of bondage. The world we see is really the world we are. We see through the mental pictures and convictions of our subconscious mind. We color everything by our inner conditioning. Man projects his feelings, prejudices, and animosities onto people and he forms a twisted, distorted picture of everything.

Define your goal now. Where are you going? What is your objective? Get a definite plan or purpose; then claim God is moving in your behalf. Whenever any negative suggestion quarrels with you relative to the goal in your mind, chop its head off incisively and decisively with your spiritual sword of reason, which tells you that there is but One Spiritual Power and that the God who gave you the desire is the same God who fulfills it. It is easy, for the "Father indwelling, He doeth the works." No one has the power to upset you or take away your faith and confidence in He Who Is. Raise your sights! Let your vision be on the goal, the summit you wish to reach, and you will go to the place where your vision is.

Become David by falling in love with God's Truths and trust completely the Infinite Wisdom to show you the solution. Know that God in action in you brings you beauty, peace, Divine right place, and harmony. David was the son of Jesse, which means the son of I Am or God. So are YOU the son of the Infinite and the child of Eternity. Draw close to your Father. He loves you and He cares for you! As you turn to Him, He will turn to you; then the dawn appears and all the shadows flee away.

THE WONDERS OF INNER SPEECH

Let the words of my mouth, and the meditation of my heart, be acceptable in thy sight, O Lord, my strength, and my redeemer.
—Psalm 19:14

WONDERS WILL HAPPEN in your life when your inner thought and feeling agree with the words of your mouth. Apropos of this I should like to cite the following case: A man was involved in a long-delayed lawsuit which had cost him considerable time, legal fees, etc. He was exasperated, bitter, and hostile toward the opposition and his own attorneys. His inner speech, which represents his inner, silent, unexpressed thoughts, was more or less as follows: "It's hopeless! This has gone on for five years; I am being sold down the river. It is useless to go on. I might as well give up," etc. I explained to him that this inner speech was highly destructive and was undoubtedly playing a major role in prolonging the case. Job said, *For the thing which I greatly feared is come upon me* (Job 3:25).

He changed his inner and outer speech completely when he fully understood what he had been doing to himself. Actually he had been praying against himself. I asked him a single question as follows: "What would you say if I told you this minute that there had been a perfect, harmonious solution reached and the whole matter was concluded?"

He replied, "I would be delighted and eternally grateful. I would feel wonderful knowing that the whole thing was finished."

He agreed from that moment on to see to it that his inner speech, as Ouspensky pointed out, would agree with his aim. Regularly and systematically he applied the following prayer which I gave him: "I give thanks for the perfect, harmonious solution which came through the wisdom of the All-Wise One." He repeated this to himself frequently during the day, and when difficulties, delays, setbacks, arguments, doubt, and fear came to his mind, he would silently affirm the above truth. He ceased completely making all negative statements verbally and also watched his inner speech, knowing that his inner speech would always be made manifest. It is what we feel on the inside that is expressed. We can say one thing with the mouth and feel another in our heart; it is what we feel that is reproduced on the screen of space. We must never affirm inwardly what we do not want to experience outwardly. The lips and the heart should agree; when they do, our prayer is answered.

We must watch our inner psychological state. Some people mutter to themselves, are envious, jealous, seething with anger and hostility. Such a mental attitude is highly destructive and brings chaos, sickness, and lack in its train. You are familiar with the person who justifies himself; he tells himself that he has a perfect right to be angry, seek revenge, and try to get even. He is playing an old subconscious phonograph record which recites all the alibis, excuses, and justification for his inner boiling state. In all probability he does not know that such a mental state causes him to lose psychic energy on a large scale, rendering him inefficient and confused. Man's negative inner speech is usually directed against some person.

I talked to a man recently who told me that he had been treated shabbily; how he planned to get even; how hateful he was toward his former employer, etc. This man had ulcers of the stomach as a result of his inner turmoil and irritation. I explained to him that he had been making very destructive impressions of anger and resentment on his subconscious mind, which always expresses what is impressed upon it. These destructive emotions must have an outlet, and they came forth as ulcers and neurosis in his case.

He reversed his mental processes by releasing his former employer into the boundless ocean of God's Love and wishing for him all the blessings of Heaven. At the same time he filled his mind with the Truths of God by identifying himself with the Infinite Healing Presence, realizing that the Harmony, Peace, and Perfection of the Infinite One were saturating his mind and body, making him every whit whole. These spiritual vibrations permeating his mind were transmitted throughout his entire system, and the cells of his body took on a new spiritual tone resulting in a healing of his discordant condition.

The Bible says, *If two of you shall agree on earth as touching anything that they shall ask, it shall be done for them of my Father which is in heaven.* Who are these two? It means you and your desire; i.e., if you accept your desire mentally, the subconscious mind will bring it to pass, because your conscious and subconscious have agreed or synchronized. The two agreeing represent your thought and feeling, your idea and emotion. If you succeed in emotionalizing the concept, the male and female aspect of your mind have agreed and there will be an issue or mental offspring, namely the answered prayer.

It must be recalled that whatever we accept or feel as true is impregnated in our subconscious mind. The subconscious is the creative medium; its tendency, as Troward points out, is always lifeward. The subconscious controls all your vital organs, is the seat of memory, and the healer of the body. The subconscious is fed by hidden springs and is one with Infinite Intelligence and Infinite Power.

It is very important to give the proper instruction to the subconscious. For example, if a man dwells on obstacles, delays, difficulties, and obstructions to his program, the subconscious will take that as his request and proceed to bring difficulties and disappointments into his experience; hence, feed the subconscious with premises which are true.

What kind of inner talking goes on in you all the time which is not being expressed audibly? It is your inner talking that the subconscious listens to and obeys. Your subconscious records your silent thought and feeling, and it is a very faithful recording machine. It records everything and plays the record back to you in the form of experiences, conditions, and events. You do not have to travel psychologically with fear, doubt, anxiety, and anger. There is no law which says that you have to travel with gangsters, assassins, murderers, intruders, and thieves in your mind. If you continue to invite such thieves and robbers into your mind, they rob you of your health, happiness, peace and prosperity, and make you a physical and mental wreck.

A woman had a blood pressure of over two hundred accompanied by severe migraine attacks; the cause of all this was destructive inner speech. She felt that someone had not treated her right and she became very negative toward that other person. She justified herself in being hostile and antagonistic toward this other person, allowing this condition to go on for weeks, and she was in a deep emotional stew. This negative attitude drained force from her, bringing about psychological changes in her bloodstream. She was ready, as she said, to explode with anger. This inner pressure, mounting tension, and seething hostility were the cause of her high blood pressure or hypertension plus the migraine.

This woman began to practice the wonders of spiritual inner speech. She realized she had been poisoning herself and that the other woman was in no way responsible for the way she was thinking or feeling about her. She was the only thinker in her universe, and she had been thinking vicious, destructive, malicious thoughts which were poisoning her whole system. She began to comprehend and see that no one could possibly touch her except through her own thought or the movement of her own mind. All she had to do in order to practice the wonders of

true spiritual inner speech was to identify with her aim. Her aim
was peace, health, happiness, joy, serenity, and tranquillity. She
began to identify with God's River of Peace and God's Love
flowing through her like a golden yellow river soothing, healing,
and restoring her mind and body.

For fifteen minutes three or four times a day she prayed silently; her inner thoughts and feelings were as follows: "God is
Love, and His Love fills my soul. God is Peace, and His Peace
fills my mind and body. God is Perfect Health, and His Health
is my Health. God is Joy, and His Joy is my Joy, and I feel wonderful." This kind of inner speech which represented her inner
thoughts of God and His qualities brought about a complete
sense of balance, poise, and harmony to her mind and body.
When the thoughts of the other woman came to her mind, she
would immediately identify with her aim—God's Peace. She
discovered the wonders of real inner speech where her lips and
heart united in identifying with the Eternal Truths of God,
thereby rendering her impermeable to the impact of negative
ideas and thoughts.

How do you meet people in your mind? That is the acid test
for the Truth which sets you free. If you meet them and see the
God in them, that is wonderful; then you are practicing the
wonders of inner speech from a constructive standpoint because
you are identifying with your aim, which is God or the good.
Ouspensky pointed out that your inner speech should always
agree with your aim.

A young man had an aim: perfect health. However, his conscious mind reminded him that he had been sick with a blood
disorder for years. He was full of anxiety, fear, and doubt. His
relatives kept reminding him that it would take a long time and
that he might never be healed. His subconscious was, of course,
receiving all these negative impressions, and he could not get a
healing. His inner speech had to agree with his aim. In other
words, the two phases of his mind had to synchronize and agree.
This young man began to talk in a different tone to his subcon-

scious. I told him as he listened carefully and avidly to affirm slowly, quietly, lovingly, and feelingly several times daily as follows: "The Creative Intelligence made my body and is creating my blood now. The Healing Presence knows how to heal and is transforming every cell of my body to God's pattern now. I hear and I see the doctor telling me that I am whole. I have this picture now in my mind, I see him clearly, I hear his voice, and he is saying to me, 'John, you're healed. It is a miracle!' I know this constructive imagery is going down into my subconscious mind where it is being developed and brought to pass. I know my subconscious mind is in touch with the Infinite One, and Its Wisdom and Power are bringing my request to pass in spite of all sensual evidence to the contrary. I feel this, I believe it, and I am now identifying with my aim—Perfect Health. This is my inner speech morning, noon, and night."

He repeated this prayer ten or fifteen minutes four or five times daily, particularly prior to sleep. Due to habit he found his mind running wild at times, fretting, fussing, worrying, recounting the verdict of others and his previous repeated failures in the healing process. When these thoughts came to his mind, he issued the order, "Stop! I am the master. All thoughts, imagery, and responses must obey me. From now on all my thoughts are on God and His Wonderful Healing Power. This is the way I feed my subconscious; I constantly identify with God, and my inner thought and feeling is 'Thank you, Father.' I do this a hundred times a day or a thousand times, if necessary."

The young man had a healing of the blood condition in three months. This is the wonder of real and true speech wherein your inner speech is the same as it would be if you had already received the answer to your prayer. *Believe that you have it now and you shall receive.* He succeeded by repetition, prayer, and meditation to get his subconscious mind to agree with his desire; then the Creative Power of God responded according to the agreement. *Thy faith hath made thee whole.*

A woman sixty-seven years of age told me all the reasons she could not get married; then she began to silently practice correct inner speech as follows: "I thank you, Father, for my perfect, ideal, divine companion." She repeated this to herself many times a day; after a while her concept was impressed on the subconscious and she met a retired druggist whom she married. They are ideally happy. Her inner speech was one with her aim. She spoke inwardly as though it had already happened. It had happened in the only place it could ever happen, namely in her own mind.

Here is an example of wrong inner speech: A member of our organization was trying to sell a house for three years. She would decree, "I release this beautiful house to Infinite Mind. I know it is sold in Divine Order to the right person at the right price, and I give thanks now that this is so." This was her prayer and there is nothing wrong with it, but she constantly neutralized it by silently saying to herself, "Times are slow, the price is too high, people don't have that kind of money. What's wrong with me? Why can't I sell it?" You can see that she was rendering her prayer null and void.

As a man thinketh in his heart so is he. Her inner speech was very negative, and that was the way she really felt about the whole matter; therefore that mental state was manifested for three years. She reversed the procedure and every night and morning she would close her eyes for five or six minutes and imagine the writer congratulating her on her sale. During the day her inner speech was: "I give thanks for the sale of my house; the buyer is prospered and blessed because of this purchase." The repetition of this phrase was impressed on her subconscious mind and made manifest. A week later a man who sat next to her in church bought her house and was very satisfied. She realized you can't go in two directions at the same time.

Let the words of my mouth, and the meditation of my heart, be acceptable in thy sight, O Lord, my strength, and my redeemer (Psalm 19:14).

Changing the Feeling of "I"

IF YOU SAY "I" to everything you think, feel, say, or imagine, you cannot transform your emotional life. Remember, all kinds of thoughts can enter your mind; all kinds of emotions may enter your heart. If you say "I" to all negative thoughts, you are identifying yourself with them. You can refuse to attach "I" to negative emotions and thoughts.

You naturally make it a practice to avoid muddy places as you walk along the road; likewise, you must avoid walking down the muddy roads of your mind where fear, resentment, hostility, and ill-will lurk and move. Refuse to listen to negative remarks. Do not touch the negative moods, nor let them touch you. Practice inner separation by getting a new feeling about yourself and about what you really are. Begin to realize that the real "I" in you is the Infinite Spirit, the Infinite One. Begin to identify yourself with the qualities and attributes of this Infinite One; then your whole life will be transformed.

The whole secret in transforming your negative emotional

nature is to practice self-observation. To observe, and specifically to *observe oneself*, are two different things. When you say, "I observe," you mean you give your attention to external things. In self-observation the attention is directed inwards.

A man may spend his whole lifetime studying the atom, stars, body, and the phenomenalistic, external world. This knowledge cannot bring about an interior change—the change of the heart.

You must learn to differentiate, to discern, to separate the chaff from the wheat. You practice the art of self-observation when you begin to ask yourself, "Is this idea true? Will it bless, heal, and inspire me? Will it give me peace of mind as well as contribute to the general well-being of humanity?"

You are living in two worlds: the external and the internal; yet they are both one. One is visible and the other invisible (objective and subjective). Your external world enters through your five senses and is shared by everyone. Your internal world of thought, feelings, sensations, beliefs, and reaction is invisible and belongs to you.

Ask yourself, "In which world do I live? Do I live only in the world revealed by my five senses or in this inner world?" It is in this inner world you live all the time; this is where you feel and suffer.

Suppose you are invited to a banquet. All you see, hear, taste, smell, and touch belongs to the external world. All that you think, feel, like, and dislike belongs to the inner world. You attend two banquets recorded differently, namely one the outer and one the inner. It is in your inner world of thought, feeling, and emotion that you rise and fall and sway to and fro.

In order to transform yourself, you must begin to change the inner world through the purification of the emotions and the correct ordering of the mind through right thinking. If you want to grow spiritually, you must transform yourself.

Transformation means the changing of one thing into another. There are many well-known transformations of matter. Sugar through a process of distillation is changed into alcohol; radium slowly changes into lead; etc. The food you eat is transformed stage by stage into all substances necessary for your existence.

Your experiences coming in as impressions must be similarly transformed. Suppose, for example, you see a person you love and admire; you receive impressions about him. Suppose on the other hand you meet a person you dislike; you receive impressions also.

Your husband or daughter sitting on the couch as you read this is to you what you conceive him or her to be. In other words, impressions are received by your mind. If you were deaf, you would not hear their voices. You can change your impressions of people. To transform your impression is to transform yourself. To change your life, change your reactions to life. Do you find yourself reacting in stereotyped ways? If your reactions are negative, that is your life. Never permit your life to be a series of negative reactions to the impressions that come to you every day.

In order truly to observe yourself, you must see that regardless of what happens, your thoughts and feelings are fixed on the great truth implied by the question, "How is it in God and Heaven?" This will lift you up and transform all your negative thoughts and emotions. You may be inclined to say that other people are to blame because of the way they talk or act, but if what they say or do makes you negative, you are inwardly disturbed; this negative state is where you now live, move, and have your being.

You cannot affort to be negative; this mental state depletes your vitality, robs you of enthusiasm, and makes you physically and mentally ill. Do you live in the room where you are now or do you live in your thoughts, feelings, emotions, hopes, and despair? Is it not what you are feeling about your environment now that is real to you? When you say, "My name is John Jones," what do you mean? Is it not a fact that you are a product of your thinking plus the customs, traditions, and the influence of those around you as you grew up? You are really the sum total of your beliefs and opinions, plus what you have derived from your education, environmental conditioning, and the countless other influences acting upon you from the external world and entering through your external senses.

Perhaps you are now comparing yourself with others. Do you feel inferior in the presence of a person who seems to be more distinguished than you are? Suppose you are a fine pianist—when someone praises another pianist, do you feel inferior? If you have the real feeling of "I," this would not be possible; for the true feeling of "I" is the feeling of the Presence of the Infinite One in you, in Which there are no comparisons.

Ouspensky used to point out that people became upset easily because their feeling of "I" was derived from negative states of consciousness. "The feeling of 'I' " was one of his favorite expressions, and some of his ideas are incorporated in this essay.

I said to a man in our Bible class recently, "Have you observed your typical reaction to people, newspaper articles, and radio commentators? Have you noticed your usual, stereotyped behaviour?"

He replied, "No, I have not noticed these things." He was taking himself for granted and not growing spiritually. He began to think about his reactions; then he admitted that many of the articles and the commentators irritated him immensely. He had been reacting in a machine-like manner and was not disciplining himself. It makes no difference if all the writers and commentators were wrong and he alone was right; the negative emotion aroused in him is destructive; it shows lack of mental and spiritual discipline.

When you say, "I think this . . . ," "I think that . . . ," "I resent this . . . ,'' or ''I dislike this . . . ,'' which ''I'' is speaking? Is it not a different ''I'' speaking every moment? Each ''I'' is completely different. One ''I'' in you criticizes one moment; a few minutes later another ''I'' speaks tenderly. Look at and learn about your different ''I's'' and know deep within yourself that certain ''I's'' will never dominate, control, or direct your thinking.

Take a good look at the ''I's'' you are consorting with. With what kind of people do you associate? I am referring to the people that inhabit your mind. Remember, your mind is a city; thoughts, ideas, opinions, feelings, sensations, and beliefs all dwell there. Some of the places in your mind are slums and dangerous streets; however, Jesus (your desire) is always walking down the streets of your mind in the form of your ideal, goal, and aim in life.

One of the meanings of Jesus is your desire; for your desire, when realized, is your saviour. Your aims and objectives in life are now beckoning to you; move toward them. Give your desire your attention; in other words, take a lively interest in it. Go down the streets of love, peace, joy, and goodwill in your mind; you will meet wonderful people on the way. You will find beautifully lighted streets and wonderful citizens on the better streets of your mind.

Never permit your house, which is your mind, to be full of servants which you do not have under control. When you were young, you were taught not to be with what your mother called ''bad company.'' Now, when you begin to awaken to your inner powers, you must make it a special point that you do not go with the wrong ''I's'' (thoughts) within you.

Every time you are prone to get angry, critical, depressed, or irritable, think of God and Heaven, and ask yourself, ''How is it in God and Heaven?'' *There* is the answer to becoming the new man; this is how you become spiritually reborn or experience what is called the second birth. (The *second birth* is internal discipline and spiritual understanding.)

The saint and the sinner are in all of us; so are the murderer and the holy man; likewise are God and the world mind. Every man basically and fundamentally wants to be good, to express good, and to do good. This is "the positive" in you. If you have committed destructive acts, as, for example, if you have robbed, cheated, and defrauded others, and they condemn you and they hold you in a bad light, you can rise out of the slum of your mind to that exalted place in your own consciousness where you cease to condemn yourself; then all your accusers must still their tongues. When you cease to accuse yourself, the world will no longer accuse you; this is the power of your own consciousness; it is the God in you.

It is foolish to condemn yourself; you do not have to. It is idle to keep company with the thoughts of self-accusation. Suppose you committed acts of injustice, criminal acts, or other dastardly actions. It was not the God in you that did those things; it was not the real "I" or the Infinite One, it was the other self (the world mind) in you. This will not, of course, excuse you from your responsibility, no more so than if you put your hand in the fire, you will get burned; or if you pass a red light, you will get a ticket for a traffic violation.

The other self represents the many "I's" in you, for instance the many negative ideas and beliefs that there are powers outside your own consciousness; the belief that others can hurt you; or that the elements are unfriendly, plus the fears, superstitions, and ignorance of all kinds. Finally, prejudices, fears, and hates drive and goad you to do that which you would not otherwise do. The ideal way to change the feeling of "I" is to affix to the real "I" within you everything that is noble, wonderful, and God-like.

Begin to affirm, "I am strong. I am radiant. I am happy. I am inspired. I am illumined. I am loving. I am kind. I am harmonious." Feel these states of mind; affirm them, and believe them; then you will begin to truly live in the garden of God. Whatever you affix to the "I AM" and believe, you become. The "I AM"

in you is God, and there is none other. "I AM" or Life, Awareness, Pure Being, Existence, or the Real Self of you is God. It is
the Only Cause. It is the Only Power making anything in the
world. Honor It; live with the feeling "I AM illumined" all day
long, and wonders will happen in your life. Feel you are inspired
from On High; continue to live in that mental atmosphere; then
you will draw out the wisdom, truth, and beauty from your
deeper mind, and your whole world will be transformed by your
inner contemplation of God's truths.

As you continue to change the feeling of "I" as outlined
above, you will populate and illuminate all the recesses of your
mind with God's eternal verities: *Fear not: for I have redeemed
thee. . . . When thou passest through the rivers, they shall not
overflow thee: when thou walkest through the fire, thou shalt
not be burned* (Isaiah 43:1,2). This is the God-Presence which
always goes before you whithersoever thou goest. Your dominant mental attitude or atmosphere is going ahead of you all the
time creating the experiences you will encounter.

Keep in mind that when you pray about any specific thing,
it is necessary to qualify your mind with the consciousness or
feeling of having or being that thing. You mentally and completely reject the arguments in your mind against it; that is
prayer. Qualify your consciousness with the thing you are praying for by thinking and deliberating about it with interest. Do
this quietly and regularly until a conviction is reached in your
consciousness. As you do this, the problem will no longer an-
noy you. You will maintain your mental poise, plus the feeling
of: "I now feel that I am what I long to be," and as you continue
to feel it, you will become it.

Here is the law: "I am that which I feel myself to be." Practice changing the feeling of "I" every day by affirming: "I am
Spirit; I think, see, feel, and live as Spirit, the Presence of God."
(The other self in you thinks, feels, and acts as the mass mind
does.) As you continue to do this, you will begin to feel that you

are one with God. As the sun in the heavens redeems the earth from darkness and gloom, so too will the realization of the Presence of God in you reveal the man you always wished to be—the joyous, radiant, peaceful, prosperous, and successful man whose intellect is illumined by the Light from above.

God causes the sun to shine on all men everywhere. No man can take away the sunshine of God's Love from you. No one can place you in the prison of fear or ignorance when you know the Truth of God which sets you free.

The feeling that the "I AM" in you is God reveals to you that there is nothing to be afraid of and that you are one with Omnipotence, Omniscience, and Omnipresence. No one can steal health, peace, joy, or happiness from you. You no longer live with the many "I's" of fear, doubt, and superstition. You now live in the Divine Presence and in the consciousness of freedom.

Ask yourself, "Who is it that takes charge of me at every moment and speaks in His Name, calling Itself 'I'?" Never identify with the negatives, such as fear, prejudice, pride, arrogance, condemnation, etc. You now realize you need not go in the direction of the negative "I's." You will never again say "Yes" to any idle, negative thought; neither will you give it the sanction and signature of yourself.

Become the observer by keeping your eyes fixed on God— the real "I"—the Infinite One within you. Feel the sense of "I" on the observing side, and not in what you are observing. Feel that you are looking out through the eyes of God; therefore, *Thou art of purer eyes than to behold evil, and canst not look on iniquity* (Habakkuk 1:13).

Stay Young
Forever

A FEW MONTHS ago I called on an old friend of mine in London who was very ill. He said to me, "We are born, grow up, become old and good-for-nothing, and that's the end." This mental attitude of futility and worthlessness was the chief reason for his sickness. He was frustrated, weak, and almost lifeless. He felt his advancing years (over 80) gave him no hope. His cry was that he was useless and that no one wanted him. He was looking forward to senescence and after that—nothing.

Unfortunately many people have the same attitude as this man. They are afraid of what they term old age, the end, and extinction, which really means that they are afraid of Life; yet Life is endless. Wisdom teaches that age is not the flight of years, but age is the dawn of wisdom. Spirit in man was never born and can never die. Spirit is God, and God hath no beginning nor end. Man's body is really the garment God wears when He takes the form of man. In order to manifest Itself, Spirit needs a form.

Man's body is the instrument through which the Spirit functions on this plane. The Spirit and the body are not separate; man's body is Spirit or Life reduced to the point of visibility. Matter and Spirit are not different—they are the same. Spirit is the highest degree of matter, and matter is the lowest degree of Spirit. Man will always have a body. When he leaves this plane, he will put on a fourth-dimensional body, and so on to infinity; for there is no end to the glory which is man's.

Life is progression; the journey is ever onward, upward, and Godward. All formed things in the universe are gradually returning to the formless, and the formless life is forever taking form. Anything that hath a beginning hath an end. Our body has a beginning; it will again return to the formless primordial substance, and we will put on a new body, for every end is a beginning.

Old age is not a tragic occurrence. What we call the aging process is change. It is to be welcomed joyfully and gladly, as each phase of human life is a step onward on the path which has no end. Man has powers which transcend his body; he has senses which transcend his five senses. Scientists today are setting forth positive, indisputable evidence that man can leave his present body and travel thousands of miles and see, hear, touch, and speak to people even though his physical body is on a couch thousands of miles away. Man's life is spiritual and eternal; he never grows old, for Spirit or Life cannot grow old. Life is self-renewing, eternal, and indestructible. God is Life, and Life is the reality of all men. The evidence of the immortality of man is overwhelming. The scientist cannot see with his eyes an electron; yet he accepts it as a scientific fact because it is the only reasonable conclusion which coincides with other observed phenomena. We can't see God or Life; however, we know we are alive. Life is, and we are here to express It in all Its beauty and glory.

The Bible says, *This is life eternal, that they might know Thee the only true God* (John 17:3). The man who thinks or believes that the earthly cycle of birth, adolescence, youth, maturity, and old age is all there is to life is indeed to be pitied; such a man has no anchor, no hope, no vision, and to him life has no meaning. This type of belief brings frustration, stagnation, cynicism, and a sense of hopelessness resulting in neurosis and mental aberrations of all kinds. If you can't play a fast game of tennis or swim as fast as your son, or if your body has slowed down, or you walk with a slow step, remember Spirit is always clothing Itself anew. What men call death is but a journey to a new city in another mansion of our Father's house.

I say to men and women in my lectures that they should accept what we call old age gracefully. Age has its own glory and beauty which belongs to it. Love, beauty, peace, joy, happiness, wisdom, goodwill, and understanding—these qualities never grow old and never die. Emerson said, "We do not count a man's years until he has nothing else to count." Your character, the quality of your mind, your faith, and convictions are not subject to decay.

I met a surgeon in England, age 84, who operates every morning, visits patients in the afternoons, and writes in the evening. He is young at 84, full of life, zeal, enthusiasm, love, and goodwill. He has not surrendered to advancing years; he knows that he is immortal. He said to me, "If I should pass on tomorrow, I would be operating on people in the next dimension, not with a surgeon's scalpel, but with mental and spiritual surgery."

John Wesley was very active in expounding his convictions about God and His laws when he was close to 90. Our own President Herbert Hoover was very active and performing monumental work on behalf of the government while in his eighties. He was healthy, happy, vigorous, and full of life and enthusiasm. I have listened to him speak over the radio; his mind was clear and decisive. I believe his mental acumen and sagacity were actually much greater then than when he was 40. He found life interesting and fascinating. I read where he spent all the time available in writing the life of former President Woodrow Wilson. Mr. Hoover was a very religious man, full of faith in God, life, and the universe. He was subjected to a barrage of criticism and condemnation in the years of the Depression, but he weathered the storm and did not grow old in hatred, resentment, illwill, and bitterness. On the contrary, he went into the silence of his soul and, communing with the Indwelling God, he found the peace which is the power at the heart of God.

The greatest of all shock absorbers and preventatives of decrepitude and mental and physical disorders is peace at the Divine Center within you. Tune in and feel it now. All the barbs, criticism, anger, and hate aimed at you will be absorbed, neutralized, and lost in the great ocean of God's love and peace within you; this is the secret of remaining young forever.

My father learned the French language at 65; became an authority on it at 70; he also made a study of Gaelic when he was over 60, and became a famous teacher of the language. He actively assisted my sister in a school of higher education and continued to do so until he passed away at 99. His mind was as clear at 99 as it was when he was 50; moreover, his handwriting and his reasoning powers had improved through the years. Cato learned Greek at 80, and Mme. Schumann-Heink reached the pinnacle of her musical success when she was a grandmother. There is an old saying which has an underlying truth: A man is as old as he feels. You are as old and as young as your thought. Reason it out for yourself. Ask yourself a simple question such as this: "When was my mind born? When will it die? Hath mind and spirit a beginning? How could there be an end to that which has no beginning or end?"

Life was never born and it will never die. Water wets it not, fire burns it not, wind blows it not away. You know these things to be true. How could you say, "I'm old, I am useless, I am un-wanted," etc.? Never in Eternity could you exhaust the glories and beauties that are within you, for Infinity is within you. There is no end to man, since there is no end to God. To main-tain this concept will keep you forever young, vital, keen, alert, alive, and full of the Light that never grows dim. Your gray hairs are a great asset to you; they symbolize wisdom, understanding, forbearance, and strength of character. Many clergymen receive all manner of wonderful offers when they are over 60; people be-lieve that they know something by that time. One man said to me recently, "The only reason I come to see you is because you have gray hairs; I believe you have been through the mill, and that you are talking from experience." Ministers find it very easy to get a good position at 45, 60, and over. A retired priest recently informed me that he has been receiving fabulous offers from many sources; he is 70. Truth, Love, and Wisdom have no age. It is possible for a boy of 12 years of age who studies the laws of mind and the way of the Spirit to have a greater knowledge of God than his grandfather who refuses to open his mind to the Truths of God.

Don't ever quit a job and say, "I am retired, I am old, I am finished." That is stagnation, death, and you *are* finished. Some men are old at 30 and others are young at 80. The mind is the masterweaver, the architect, the designer, and the sculptor. George Bernard Shaw was quite active at 90, and the architec-tural quality of his mind had not relaxed from active duty. I meet men and women who tell me that some employers almost slam the door in their faces when they say that they are over 40. This attitude on the part of these employers is to be considered cold, callous, evil, and completely void of compassion or under-standing. The total emphasis seems to be on youth, i.e. you must be under 35.

The reasoning behind this is certainly very shallow. If the employer would stop and think, he would realize that the applicant was not selling his age or gray hair; rather he was willing to give of his talents, his experience, his wisdom gathered through years of experience in the marketplace of life. By means of practice and application, the person's age should be a distinct asset to the organization. His gray hair, if he has any, should stand for greater wisdom, skill, and understanding. A man or woman with emotional and spiritual maturity is a tremendous blessing to any organization. A person should not be asked to resign when he is 65; that is the time of life when he could be most useful in handling personnel problems, making plans for the future, shaping decisions, and acting in the realm of creative ideas based on his experience and insight into the nature of the business.

A motion-picture writer in Hollywood told me that he had to write scripts which would cater to the 12-year-old mind. This is a tragic state of affairs, which indicates that the great masses of people have not become emotionally and spiritually mature. It means that all the accent is placed on youth, and youth stands for inexperience, lack of discernment, and hasty judgment. I am now thinking of a man of 60 who is trying frantically to keep young. He swims with young men every Sunday, goes on long hikes, plays tennis, and boasts of his prowess and physical powers, saying, "Look, I can keep up with the best of them," etc. He has forgotten the great truth: *As a man thinketh in his heart, so is he.* Diets, exercise, and games of all kinds will not keep this man young. It is necessary for him to see that he grows old or young through his processes of thinking. The Spirit is conditioned by thought; if his thoughts are on the beautiful, the noble, and the good, he will be young regardless of his chronological years.

Job said, "The thing which I greatly feared is come upon me." There are many people who fear old age and are uncertain about the future, expecting mental and physical deterioration as the years advance. What they think and feel comes to pass. We grow old when we lose interest in life, when we cease to dream, to hunger after new truths and worlds to conquer. When the mind is open to new ideas, new interests, and when we raise the curtain and let in the sunshine and inspiration of new truths of God and His universe, we will always be young and vital. If you are 90 or 99, realize you have much to give. You can help stabilize, guide, and direct the younger generation; you can give of your knowledge, your experience, and your wisdom; you can always look ahead, for you are gazing into Infinity. You will find that you can never cease to unveil the glories and the wonders of the Infinite One. Veil after veil is lifted, and Its Face becomes more august and wonderful. Try to learn something new every moment of the day and you will find your mind will always be young.

I was introduced to a man in Bombay who said he was 110 years old; he had the most beautiful face I have ever seen. He seemed transfigured by the radiance of an inner light. There was a rare beauty in his eyes indicating he had grown old with gladness.

I receive many letters from men and women who say, "I was turned down because I am over 40." This is a stupid indifference to the sincere desire of these workers to express their talents and abilities. It would seem that we have created a new cult called the "Thirty-five Cult." One man told me that he could not be hired because he was 36 and the company would have to pay a few dollars more for insurance premiums. How narrow-minded, short-sighted, and revolting is such an attitude! The reverse should be true. There should be a respect for the man's experience and capacities.

The newspapers are taking cognizance of the fact that the voting population of the elderly in California elections is increasing by leaps and bounds; this means their voice will be heard in the legislature of the state and also in the halls of Congress. I believe there should be a federal law enacted prohibiting employers from discriminating against men and women just because of age. A man of 65 may be younger mentally, psychologically, and physically than many men at 30. It is stupid and ridiculous beyond words to tell a man he can't be hired because he is over 40. It is like saying to him that he is ready for the scrap heap or the junk pile. What is a man of 40 or over to do— bury his talents and hide his light under a bushel? Men who are deprived and prevented from working because of age must be sustained by government treasuries at county, state, and federal levels; the very organizations who refused to hire them and benefit from their wisdom and experience will be taxed to support them. They are biting off their nose to spite their face; it is a form of financial suicide.

Man is here to enjoy the fruit of his labor and is here to be a producer and not the prisoner of a society which compels him to idleness. Man's body slows down gradually as he advances through the years, but the mind can be much more active, alert, alive, and quickened by the Holy Spirit. Man's mind does not have to grow old. Job said, *Oh that I were as in months past, as in the days when God preserved me; when his candle shined upon my head, and when by his light I walked through darkness; as I was in the days of my youth, when the secret of God was upon my tabernacle* (Job 29:2-4).

The secret which Job speaks of is Joy. All of us can capture our youth by stirring up the gift of God within us. Every time we recognize the Spirit within as Lord Omnipotent and reject the power of false beliefs of the world, we are stirring up the gift of God within us. *In Him there is fulness of Joy. The joy of the Lord is my strength.*

Feel the Miraculous, Healing, Self-Renewing, Ever-Living God moving through your mind and body. Know that you are inspired, lifted up, rejuvenated, and strengthened; then you will feel a deep response and become rejuvenated, revitalized, and recharged spiritually. You can bubble over with enthusiasm and joy as in the days of your youth for the simple reason that you can always recapture the joyous state mentally and emotionally. The candle which shines upon your head is Divine Intelligence which reveals to you everything you need to know and enables you to affirm the presence of your good regardless of appearances. You walk by His Light, because you know the dawn appears and all the shadows flee away.

Instead of saying, "I am old," say, "I am wise in the ways of God." You are never a failure, for you know "He never faileth." You can always travel in your mind and conquer new fields. Don't let the race mind, corporations, newspapers, statistics hold a picture before you of old age, declining years, decrepitude, senility, and uselessness. Reject it, for it is a lie. You can rise above the race mind and refuse to be hypnotized by such propaganda. Affirm Life—not death. Realize you live forever, and Spirit is your reality. Get a vision of yourself as happy, radiant, successful, serene, and full of the Light of God. If you are retired, get interested in the Bible, its inner meaning. Get a new vocation, do something you always loved to do. Go to the university and take up subjects you always wanted to study. Travel, explore, investigate, and pray as follows: *As the hart panteth after the water brooks, so panteth my soul after thee, O God* (Psalm 42:1).

Be sure that your mind never retires. It must be like a parachute, which is no good except it opens up. Be open and receptive to new ideas. I have seen men of 65 and 70 retire; they seem to rot away and in a few months pass on; they felt life was at an end. This retirement was a new venture, a new challenge, a new path, the beginning of the fulfillment of a long dream. It is inexpressibly depressing to hear a man say, "What shall I do? I'm retired!" He is saying in effect, "I am mentally and physically dead. My mind is bankrupt of ideas." All this is a false picture. The real truth is you can accomplish more at 90 than you did at 60, because each day you are growing in wisdom and understanding of God and His universe through your new studies and interest.

His flesh shall be fresher than a child's: he shall return to the days of his youth (Job 33:25). Realize you will never have an old mind except you think you have. Learn to give all allegiance and devotion to the Indwelling God which is supreme, the only Cause and Power. To give power to the race mind, to senescence, sickness, to people, conditions, and events divides your allegiance and instills conflict and fear. You might be 80 years chronologically speaking, but if you are cranky, irritable, irascible, petulant, and cantankerous, you are really old regardless of the number of years you have accumulated, whether 30 or 90. Old age means the contemplation of the truth of God from the highest standpoint. This brings you to the well of God where you drink of the waters of life which keep you forever refreshed and God-intoxicated.

Look forward to a greater degree of spiritual awareness and realize that you are on an endless journey, a series of infinite advances in the ceaseless, tireless, endless ocean of God's Love; then with the Psalmist you will say, *They shall still bring forth fruit in old age; they shall be fat and flourishing* (Psalm 92:14). *The fruit of the Spirit is love, joy, peace, patience, gentleness, goodness, faith, meekness, temperance: against such there is no law* (Gal. 5:22, 23).

You are a son of the Infinite which knows no end, and you are a child of Eternity.

How to Attract Money

YOUR RIGHT TO BE RICH

IT IS YOUR RIGHT to be rich. You are here to lead the abundant life and to be happy, radiant, and free. You should, therefore, have all the money you need to lead a full, happy, prosperous life.

There is no virtue in poverty; the latter is a mental disease, and it should be abolished from the face of the earth. You are here to grow, expand, and unfold—spiritually, mentally, and materially. You have the inalienable right to fully develop and express yourself along all lines. You should surround yourself with beauty and luxury.

Why be satisfied with just enough to go around when you can enjoy the riches of the Infinite? In this book you will learn to make friends with money, and you will always have a surplus. Your desire to be rich is a desire for a fuller, happier, more wonderful life. It is a cosmic urge. It is good and very good.

Begin to see money in its true significance: as a symbol of exchange. It means to you freedom from want; it means beauty, luxury, abundance, and refinement.

As you read this chapter, you are probably saying, "I want more money." "I am worthy of a higher salary than I am receiving."

I believe most people are inadequately compensated. One of the reasons many people do not have more money is that they are silently or openly condemning it. They refer to money as "filthy lucre," or they believe that "Love of money is the root of all evil," etc. Another reason they do not prosper is that they have a sneaky, subconscious feeling there is some virtue in poverty; this subconscious pattern may be due to early childhood training, superstition, or it could be based on a false interpretation of the Scriptures.

There is no virtue in poverty; it is a disease like any other mental disease. If you were physically ill, you would think there was something wrong with you; you would seek help, or do something about the condition at once. Likewise, if you do not have money constantly circulating in your life, there is something radically wrong with you.

Money is only a symbol; it has taken many forms as a medium of exchange down through the centuries, such as salt, beads, and trinkets of various kinds. In early times, man's wealth was determined by the number of sheep or oxen he had. It is much more convenient to write a check than to carry some sheep around with you to pay your bills.

God does not want you to live in a hovel or to go hungry. God *wants* you to be happy, prosperous, and successful. God is always successful in all His undertakings, whether He makes a star or a cosmos!

You may wish to take a trip around the world, study art in foreign countries, go to college, or send your children to a superior school. You certainly wish to bring up your children in lovely surroundings, so that they might learn to appreciate beauty, order, symmetry, and proportion.

You were born to succeed, to win, to conquer all difficulties, and to have all your faculties fully developed. If there is financial lack in your life, do something about it.

Get away immediately from all superstitious beliefs about money. Do not ever regard money as evil or filthy. If you do, you cause it to take wings and fly away from you. Remember that you lose what you condemn.

Suppose, for example, you found gold, silver, lead, copper, or iron in the ground. Would you pronounce these things evil? God pronounced all things good. The evil comes from man's darkened understanding, from his unillumined mind, from his false interpretation of life and his misuse of Divine Power. Uranium, lead, or some other metal could have been used as a medium of exchange. We use paper bills, checks, etc.; surely the piece of paper is not evil; neither is the check. Physicists and scientists know today that the only difference between one metal and another is the number and rate of motion of the electrons revolving around a central nucleus. They are now changing one metal into another through a bombardment of the atoms in the powerful cyclotron. Gold under certain conditions becomes mercury. It will be only a little while until gold, silver, and other metals will be made synthetically in the chemical laboratory. I cannot imagine seeing anything evil in electrons, neutrons, protons, and isotopes.

The piece of paper in your pocket is composed of electrons and protons arranged differently; their number and rate of motion is different; that is the only way the paper differs from the silver in your pocket.

Some people will say, "Oh, people kill for money! They steal for money!" It has been associated with countless crimes, but that does not make it evil.

A man may give another $5000 to kill someone; he has misused money in using it for a destructive purpose. You can use electricity to kill someone or to light the house. You can use water to quench the baby's thirst or to drown the child. You can use fire to warm the child or burn it to death.

Another illustration would be if you brought some earth from your garden and put it in your coffee cup for breakfast: that would be your evil; yet the earth is not evil; neither is the coffee. The earth is misplaced; it belongs in your garden.

Similarly, if a needle were stuck in your thumb, it would be your evil; the needle or pin belongs in the pin cushion, not in your thumb.

We know that the forces or the elements of nature are not evil; it depends on our use of them whether they bless or hurt us.

A man said to me once, "I am broke. I do not like money; it is the root of all evil."

Love of money to the exclusion of everything else will cause you to become lopsided and unbalanced. You are here to use your power or authority wisely. Some men crave power; others crave money. If you set your heart on money, and say, "That is all I want. I am going to give all my attention to amassing money; nothing else matters," you can get money and attain a fortune, but you have forgotten that you are here to lead a balanced life. "Man does not live by bread alone."

For example, if you belong to some cult, or religious group, and become fanatical about it, excluding yourself from your friends, society, and social activities, you will become unbalanced, inhibited, and frustrated. Nature insists on a balance. If all your time is devoted to external things and possessions, you will find yourself hungry for peace of mind, harmony, love, joy, or perfect health. You will find that you cannot buy anything that is real. You can amass a fortune, or have millions of dollars; this is not evil or bad. Love of money to the exclusion of everything else results in frustration, disappointment, and disillusionment; in that sense it is the root of your evil.

By making money your sole aim, you simply made a wrong choice. You thought that was all you wanted, but you found after all your efforts that it was not only the money you needed. What you really desired was true place, peace of mind, and abundance. You could have the million or many millions, if you wanted them, and still have peace of mind, harmony, perfect health, and Divine expression.

Everyone wants enough money, and not just enough to go around. He wants abundance and to spare; he should have it. The urges, desires, and impulses we have for food, clothing, homes, better means of transportation, expression, procreation, and abundance are all God-given, Divine, and good, but we may misdirect these impulses, desires, and urges, resulting in evil or negative experiences in our lives.

Man does not have an evil nature; there is no evil nature in you; it is God, the Universal Wisdom, or Life seeking expression through you.

For example, a boy wants to go to college, but he does not have enough money. He sees other boys in the neighborhood going off to college and the university; his desire increases. He says to himself, "I want an education, too." Such a youth may steal or embezzle money for the purpose of going to college. The desire to go to college was basically and fundamentally good; he misdirected that desire or urge by violating the laws of society, the cosmic law of harmony, or the Golden Rule; then he finds himself in trouble.

However, if this boy knew the laws of mind and his unqualified capacity through the use of the Spiritual Power to go to college, he would be free and not in jail. Who put him in jail? He placed himself there. The policeman who locked him up in prison was an instrument of the man-made laws which he violated. He first imprisoned himself in his mind by stealing and hurting others. Fear and a guilt consciousness followed; this is the prison of the mind, followed by the prison walls made of bricks and stones.

Money is a symbol of God's opulence, beauty, refinement, and abundance, and it should be used wisely, judiciously, and constructively to bless humanity in countless ways. It is merely a symbol of the economic health of the nation. When your blood is circulating freely, you are healthy. When money is circulating freely in your life, you are economically healthy. When people begin to hoard money, to put it away in tin boxes, and become charged with fear, there is economic illness.

The crash of 1929 was a psychological panic; it was fear seizing the minds of people everywhere. It was a sort of negative, hypnotic spell.

You are living in a subjective and objective world. You must not neglect the spiritual food, such as peace of mind, love, beauty, harmony, joy, and laughter.

Knowledge of the spiritual power is the means to the Royal Road to Riches of all kinds, whether your desire is spiritual, mental, or material. The student of the laws of mind, or the student of the spiritual principle, believes and knows absolutely that regardless of the economic situation, stock-market fluctuation, depression, strikes, war, or other conditions and circumstances, he will always be amply supplied regardless of what form money may take. The reason for this is that he abides in the consciousness of wealth. The student has convinced himself in his mind that wealth is forever flowing freely in his life and there is always a Divine surplus. Should there be a war tomorrow and all the student's present holdings become valueless, as the German marks did after the First World War, he would still attract wealth and be cared for, regardless of the form the new currency took.

Wealth is a state of consciousness; it is a mind conditioned to Divine supply forever flowing. The scientific thinker looks at money or wealth like the tide, i.e. it goes out, but it always

comes back. The tides never fail; neither will man's supply
when he trusts a tireless, changeless, immortal Presence which
is Omnipresent and flowing ceaselessly. The man who knows
the workings of the subconscious mind is never, therefore,
worried about the economic situation, stock-market panics,
devaluation, or inflation of currency, since he abides in the consciousness of God's eternal supply. Such a man is always supplied and watched over by an overshadowing Presence. "Behold
the birds of the air: for they sow not, neither do they reap, nor
gather into barns; yet your heavenly Father feedeth them. Are
you not much better than they?"

As you consciously commune with the Divine Presence,
claiming and knowing that It leads and guides you in all your
ways, that It is a Lamp unto your feet, and a Light on your path,
you will be Divinely prospered and sustained beyond your
wildest dreams.

Here is a simple way for you to impress your subconscious
mind with the idea of constant supply or wealth: Quiet the
wheels of your mind. Relax! Let go! Immobilize the attention.
Get into a sleepy, drowsy, meditative state of mind; this reduces
effort to the minimum; then, in a quiet, relaxed, passive way,
reflect on simple truths by asking yourself: Where do ideas come
from? Where does wealth come from? Where did I come from?
Where did my brain and my mind come from? You will be led
back to the One Source.

You find yourself on a spiritual, working basis now. It will
no longer insult your intelligence to realize that wealth is a state
of mind. Take this little phrase; repeat it slowly four or five
minutes three or four times a day quietly to yourself, particularly before you go to sleep: "Money is forever circulating freely
in my life, and there is always a Divine surplus." As you do this
regularly and systematically, the idea of wealth will be conveyed
to your deeper mind, and you will develop a wealth consciousness. Idle, mechanical repetition will not succeed in building

the consciousness of wealth. Begin to feel the truth of what you affirm. You know what you are doing, and why you are doing it. You know your deeper self is responsive to what you consciously accept as true.

In the beginning, people who are in financial difficulties do not get results with such affirmations as, "I am wealthy," "I am prosperous," "I am successful"; such statements may cause their conditions to get worse. The reason is the subconscious mind will accept only the dominant of two ideas, or the dominant mood or feeling. When they say, "I am prosperous," their feeling of lack is greater, and something within them says, "No, you are not prosperous; you are broke." The feeling of lack is dominant, so that each affirmation calls forth the mood of lack, and more lack becomes theirs. The way to overcome this for beginners is to affirm what the conscious and subconscious mind will agree on; then there will be no contradiction. Our subconscious mind accepts our beliefs, feelings, convictions, and what we consciously accept as true.

A man could engage the cooperation of his subconscious mind by saying, "I am prospering every day." "I am growing in wealth and in wisdom every day." "Every day my wealth is multiplying." "I am advancing, growing, and moving forward financially." These and similar statements would not create any conflict in the mind.

For instance, if a salesman has only ten cents in his pocket, he can easily agree that he could have more tomorrow. If he sold a pair of shoes tomorrow, there is nothing within him which says his sales could not increase. He could use statements, such as, "My sales are increasing every day." "I am advancing and moving forward." He would find these would be sound psychologically and acceptable to his mind, and they would produce desirable fruit.

The spiritually advanced students who quietly, knowingly, and feelingly say, "I am prosperous," "I am successful," "I am wealthy," get wonderful results also. Why would this be true? When they think, feel, or say, "I am prosperous," they mean God is All Supply or Infinite Riches, and what is true of God is true of them. When they say, "I am wealthy," they know God is Infinite Supply, the Inexhaustible Treasure-House, and what is true of God is, therefore, true of them, for God is within them.

Many men get wonderful results by dwelling on three abstract ideas, such as health, wealth, and success. *Health* is a Divine Reality or quality of God. *Wealth* is of God; it is eternal and endless. *Success* is of God; God is always successful in all His undertakings.

The way they produce remarkable results is to stand before a mirror as they shave, and repeat for five or ten minutes: "Health, wealth, and success." They do not say, "I am healthy," or "I am successful;" they create no opposition in their minds. They are quiet and relaxed; thus the mind is receptive and passive; then they repeat these words. Amazing results follow. All they are doing is identifying with truths that are eternal, changeless, and timeless.

You can develop a wealth consciousness. Put the principles enunciated and elaborated on in this book to practice, and your desert will rejoice and blossom as the rose.

I worked with a young boy in Australia many years ago who wanted to become a physician and surgeon, but he had no money; nor had he graduated from high school. For expenses, he used to clean doctors' offices, wash windows, and do odd repair jobs. He told me that every night as he went to sleep, he used to see a diploma on a wall with his name in big, bold letters. He used to clean and shine the diplomas in the medical building where he worked; it was not hard for him to engrave the diploma in his mind and develop it there. I do not know how long he continued this imaging, but it must have been for some months.

Results followed as he persisted. One of the doctors took a great liking to this young boy, who, after being trained in the art of sterilizing instruments, giving hypodermic injections, and other miscellaneous first-aid work, became a technical assistant in his office. The doctor sent him to high school and also to college at his own expense.

Today this man is a prominent doctor in Montreal. He had a dream! A clear image in his mind! *His wealth was in his mind.*

Wealth is your idea, desire, talent, urge for service, capacity to give to mankind, your ability for usefulness to society, and your love for humanity in general.

This young boy operated a great law unconsciously. Troward says, ''Having seen the end, you have willed the means to the realization of the end.'' The *end* in this boy's case was to be a physician. To imagine, see, and feel the reality of being a doctor now, to live with that idea, sustain it, nourish it, and to love it until through his imagination it penetrated the layers of the subconscious, became a conviction and paved the way to the fulfillment of his dreams.

He could have said, ''I have no education.'' ''I do not know the right people.'' ''I am too old to go to school now.'' ''I have no money; it would take years, and I am not intelligent.'' He would then be beaten before he started. His wealth was in his use of the Spiritual Power within him which responded to his thought.

The means or the way in which our prayer is answered is always hidden from us, except that occasionally we may intuitively perceive a part of the process. ''My ways are past finding out.'' The *ways* are not known. The only thing man has to do is to imagine and accept the end in his mind, and leave its unfoldment to the subjective wisdom within.

Oftentimes the question is asked, ''What should I do after meditating on the end and accepting my desire in consciousness?'' The answer is simple: You will be compelled to do whatever is necessary for the unfoldment of your ideal. The law of the subconscious is compulsion. The law of life is action and reaction. What we do is the automatic response to our inner movements of the mind, inner feeling, and conviction.

A few months ago as I went to sleep, I imagined I was reading one of my most popular essays, *Magic of Faith*,* in French. I began to realize and imagine this book going into all French-speaking nations. For several weeks I did this every night, falling asleep with the imaginary French edition of *Magic of Faith* in my hands.

Just before Christmas, 1954, I received a letter from a leading publisher in Paris, enclosing a contract drawn up, asking me to sign it, giving him permission to publish and promote abroad to all French-speaking countries the French edition of *Magic of Faith*.

You might ask me what did I do about the publishing of this book after prayer? I would have to say, "Nothing!" The subjective wisdom took over and brought it to pass in its own way, which was a far better way than any method I could consciously devise.

All of our external movements, motions, and actions follow the inner movements of the mind. Inner action precedes all outer action. Whatever steps you take physically, or what you seem to do objectively, will all be a part of a pattern which you were compelled to fulfill.

Accepting the end wills the means to the realization of the end. Believe that you have it now, and you shall receive it.

We must cease denying our good. Realize that the only thing that keeps us from the riches that lie all around us is our mental attitude, or the way we look at God, life, and the world in general. Know, believe, and act on the positive assumption that there is no reason why you cannot have, be, and do whatever you wish to accomplish through the great laws of God.

*See p. 124.

Your knowledge of how your mind works is your saviour and redeemer. Thought and feeling are your destiny. You possess everything by right of consciousness. The consciousness of health produces health; the consciousness of wealth produces wealth. The world seems to deny or oppose what you pray for; your senses sometimes mock and laugh at you.

If you say to your friend that you are opening up a new business for yourself, he may proceed to give you all the reasons why you are bound to fail. If you are susceptible to his hypnotic spell, he may instill fear of failure in your mind. As you become aware of the spiritual power which is one and indivisible, and which responds to your thought, you will reject the darkness and ignorance of the world and know that you possess all the equipment, power, and knowledge to succeed.

To walk on the Royal Road to Riches, you must not place obstacles and impediments on the pathway of others; neither must you be jealous or envious of others. Actually, when you entertain these negative states of mind, you are hurting and injuring yourself, because you are thinking and feeling it. As Quimby said, "The suggestion you give to another, you are giving to yourself." This is the reason that the law of the golden rule is a cosmic, Divine law.

I am sure you have heard men say, "That fellow has a racket." "He is a racketeer." "He is getting money dishonestly." "He is a faker." "I knew him when he had nothing." "He is crooked, a thief, and a swindler." If you analyze the man who talks like that, he is usually in want or suffering from some financial or physical illness. Perhaps his former college friends went up the ladder of success and excelled him; now he is bitter and envious of their progress. In many instances this is the cause of his downfall. Thinking negatively of these classmates, and condemning their wealth, causes the wealth and prosperity he is praying for to vanish and flee away. He is condemning the things he is praying for. He is praying two ways. On the one hand he is saying, "God is prospering me," and in the next breath, silently or audibly, he is saying, "I resent that fellow's wealth." Always make it a special point to bless the other person, and rejoice in his prosperity and success; when you do, you bless and prosper yourself.

If you go into the bank and you see your competitor across the street deposit twenty times more than you do, or you see him deposit $10,000, rejoice and be exceedingly glad to see God's abundance being manifested through one of his sons. You are then blessing and exalting what you are praying for. What you bless, you multiply. What you condemn, you lose.

If you are working in a large organization, and you are silently thinking of and resenting the fact that you are underpaid, that you are not appreciated, and that you deserve more money and greater recognition, you are subconsciously severing your ties with that organization. You are setting a law in motion; then the superintendent or manager says to you, "We have to let you go." You dismissed yourself. The manager was simply the instrument through which your own negative mental state was confirmed. In other words, he was a messenger telling you what you conceived as true about yourself. It was an example of the law of action and reaction. The action was the internal movement of your mind; the *reaction* was the response of the outer world to conform to your inner thinking.

Perhaps as you read this you are thinking of someone who has prospered financially by taking advantage of others, by defrauding them, by selling them unsound investments in property, etc. The answer to this is obvious, because if we rob, cheat, or defraud another, we do the same to ourselves. In reality, in this case we are actually hurting or robbing from ourselves. We are in a mood of lack in the first place, which is bound to attract loss to us. The loss may come in many ways; it may come in loss of health, prestige, peace of mind, social status, sickness in the home, or in business. It may not necessarily come in loss of money. We must not be shortsighted and think that the loss has to come in just dollars and cents.

Isn't it a wonderful feeling to place your head on the pillow at night and feel you are at peace with the whole world, and that your heart is full of goodwill toward all? There are some people who have accumulated money the wrong way—by trampling on others, trickery, deceit, and chicanery. What is the price? Sometimes it is mental and physical disease, guilt complexes, insomnia, or hidden fears. As one man said to me, "Yes, I rode roughshod over others. I got what I wanted, but I got cancer doing it." He realized he had attained his wealth in the wrong way.

You can be wealthy and prosperous without hurting anyone. Many men are constantly robbing themselves; they steal from themselves: peace of mind, health, joy, inspiration, happiness, and the laughter of God. They may say that they have never stolen, but is it true? Every time we resent another, or are jealous or envious of another's wealth or success, we are stealing from ourselves. These are the thieves and robbers which Jesus cast out of the temple; likewise, you must cast them out incisively and decisively. Do not let them live in your mind. Cut their heads off with the fire of right thought and feeling.

I remember in the early days of World War II reading about a woman in Brooklyn, New York, who went around from store to store buying up all the coffee she could. She knew it was going to be rationed; she was full of fear that there would not be enough for her. She bought as much as she could and stored it in the cellar. That evening she went to church services. When she came home, burglars had broken down the door and stolen not only the coffee, but silverware, money, jewelry, and other things.

This good woman said what they all say: "Why did this happen to me when I was at church? I never stole from anyone."

Is it true? Was she not in the consciousness of lack and fear when she began to hoard supplies of coffee? Her mood and fear of lack were sufficient to bring about loss in her home and possessions. She did not have to put her hand in the cash register or rob a bank; her fear of lack produced lack. This is the reason that many people who are what society calls "good citizens" suffer loss. They are good in the worldly sense, i.e. they pay their taxes; they obey the laws, vote regularly, and are generous to charities; but they are resentful of others' possessions, wealth, or social position. If they would like to take money when no one was looking, such an attitude is definitely and positively a state of lack and may cause the person who indulges in such a mental state to attract charlatans or knaves who may swindle or cheat him in some business transaction.

Before the outer thief robs us, we have first robbed ourselves. There must be an inner thief before the outer one appears.

A man can have a guilt complex and accuse himself constantly. I knew such a man; he was very honest as a teller in a bank. He never stole any money, but he had an illicit romance; he was supporting another woman, and denying his family. He lived in fear that he would be discovered; a deep sense of guilt resulted. Fear follows guilt. Fear causes a contraction of the muscles and mucous membranes; acute sinusitis developed. Medication gave him only temporary relief.

I explained to this client the cause of his trouble and told him the cure was to give up his outside affair. He said he couldn't; he had tried, but she was his soul mate. He was always condemning and accusing himself.

One day he was accused by one of the officers of the bank of having embezzled some money; it looked serious for him, as the evidence was circumstantial. He became panic-stricken and realized that the only reason he was wrongfully accused was that he had been accusing and condemning himself. He saw how mind operates. Inasmuch as he was always accusing himself on the inner plane, he would be accused on the outer.

He immediately broke off the relationship with the other woman due to the shock of being accused of embezzling and began to pray for Divine harmony and understanding between himself and the bank officer. He began to claim, "There is nothing hidden that is not revealed. The peace of God reigns supreme in the minds and hearts of all concerned."

Truth prevailed. The whole matter was dissolved in the light of truth. Another young man was discovered as the culprit. The bank teller knew that only through prayer was he saved from a jail sentence.

The great law is, "As you would that men should think about you, think you about them in the same manner. As you would that men should feel about you, feel you also about them in like manner."

Say from your heart, "I wish for every man who walks the earth, what I wish for myself. The sincere wish of my heart is, therefore, peace, love, joy, abundance, and God's blessings to all men everywhere." Rejoice and be glad in the progression, advancement, and prosperity of all men. Whatever you claim as true for yourself, claim it for all men everywhere. If you pray for happiness and peace of mind, let your claim be peace and happiness for all. Do not ever try to deprive another of any joy. If you do, you deprive yourself. When the ship comes in for your friend, it comes in for you also.

If someone is promoted in your organization, be glad and happy. Congratulate him, rejoice in his advancement and recognition. If you are angry or resentful, you are demoting yourself. Do not try to withhold from another his God-given birthright to happiness, success, achievement, abundance, and all good things.

Jesus said, "Store up for yourselves treasures in heaven, where the moth and the rust do not consume, and where thieves cannot break through and steal." Hatred and resentment rot and corrode the heart, causing us to become full of scars, impurities, toxins, and poisons.

The treasures of heaven are the truths of God which we possess in our soul. Fill your minds with peace, harmony, faith, joy, honesty, integrity, loving-kindness, and gentleness; then you will be sowing for yourself treasures in the heavens of your own mind.

If you are seeking wisdom regarding investments, or if you are worried about your stocks or bonds, quietly claim, "Infinite Intelligence governs and watches over all my financial transactions, and whatsoever I do shall prosper." Do this frequently and you will find that your investments will be wise; moreover, you will be protected from loss, as you will be prompted to sell your securities or holdings before any loss accrues to you.

Let the following prayer be used daily by you regarding your home, business, and possessions: "The overshadowing Presence which guides the planets on their course and causes the sun to shine watches over all my possessions, home, business, and all things that are mine. God is my fortress and vault. All my possessions are secure in God. It is wonderful." By reminding yourself daily of this great truth, and by observing the laws of Love, you will always be guided, watched over, and prospered in all your ways. You will never suffer from loss, for you have chosen the Most High as your Counselor and Guide. The envelope of God's Love surrounds, enfolds, and encompasses you at all times. You rest in the Everlasting Arms of God.

All of us should seek an inner guidance for our problems. If you have a financial problem, repeat this before you retire at night: "Now I shall sleep in peace. I have turned this matter over to the God-Wisdom within. It knows only the answer. As the sun rises in the morning, so will my answer be resurrected. I know the sunrise never fails." Then go off to sleep.

Do not fret, fuss, and fume over a problem. Night brings counsel. Sleep on it. Your intellect cannot solve all your problems. Pray for the Light that is to come. Remember that the dawn always comes; then the shadows flee away. Let your sleep every night be a contented bliss.

You are not a victim of circumstances except you believe you are. You can rise and overcome any circumstance or condition. You will have different experiences as you stand on the rock of spiritual Truth, steadfast, and faithful to your deeper purposes and desires.

In large stores, the management employs store detectives to prevent people from stealing; they catch a number every day trying to get something for nothing. All such people are living in the consciousness of lack and limitation, and they are stealing from themselves, attracting at the same time all manner of loss. These people lack faith in God and the understanding of how their minds work. If they would pray for true place, Divine expression, and supply, they would find work; then by honesty, integrity, and perseverance they would become a credit to themselves and society at large.

Jesus said, "For ye have the poor always with you; but me ye have not always." The *poor states* of consciousness are always with us in this sense, that no matter how much wealth you now have, there is something you want with all your heart. It may be a problem of health; perhaps a son or daughter needs guidance, or harmony is lacking in the home. At that moment you are poor.

We could not know what abundance was except we were conscious of lack. "I have chosen twelve, and one of you is a devil."

Whether it be the King of England or the boy in the slums, we are all born into limitation and into the race belief. It is through these limitations we grow. We could never discover the Inner Power except through problems and difficulties; these are our *poor states* which prod us in seeking the solution. We could not know what joy was except we could shed a tear of sorrow. We must be aware of poverty to seek liberation and freedom, and to ascend into God's opulence.

The *poor states*, such as fear, ignorance, worry, lack, and pain, are not bad when they cause you to seek the opposite.

When you get into trouble and are kicked from pillar to post; when you ask negative, heart-rending questions, such as "Why are all these things happening to me? Why does there seem to be a jinx following me?" light will come into your mind. Through your suffering, pain, or misery you will discover the truth which sets you free. "Sweet are the uses of adversity, like a toad ugly and venomous, yet wears a precious jewel on its head."

Through dissatisfaction we are led to satisfaction. All those studying the laws of life have been dissatisfied with something. They have had some problem or difficulty which they could not solve; or they were not satisfied with the man-made answers to life's riddles. They have found their answer in the God-Presence within themselves—the pearl of great price, the precious jewel. The Bible says, "I sought the Lord, and I found him, and He delivered me from all my fears."

When you realize your ambition or desire, you will be satisfied for only a brief period of time; then the urge to expand will come again. This is Life seeking to express Itself at higher levels through you. When one desire is satisfied, another comes, and so on to infinity. You are here to grow. Life is progression; it is not static. You are here to go from glory to glory; there is no end; for there is no end to God's glory.

We are all poor in the sense that we are forever seeking more light, wisdom, happiness, and greater joy out of life. God is Infinite, and never in eternity could you exhaust the glory, beauty, and wisdom which is within; this is how wonderful you are.

In the absolute state all things are finished, but in the relative world we must awaken to that glory which was ours before the world was. No matter how wise you are, you are seeking more wisdom; so you are still poor. No matter how intelligent you are in the field of mathematics, physics, or astronomy, you are only scratching the surface. You are still poor. The journey is ever onward, upward, and Godward. It is really an awakening process, whereby you realize creation is finished. When you know God does not have to learn, grow, expand, or unfold, you begin to gradually awaken from the dream of limitation and become alive in God. As the scales of fear, ignorance, race belief, and mass hypnosis fall from your eyes, you begin to see as God sees. The blind spots are removed; then you begin to see the world as God made it; for we begin to see it through God's eyes. Now you say, "Behold, the Kingdom of Heaven is at hand!"

Feed the "poor" within you; clothe the naked ideas, and give them form by believing in the reality of the idea, trusting the great Fabricator within to clothe it in form and objectify it. Now your word (idea) shall become flesh (take form). When you are hungry (poor states), you seek food. When worried, you seek peace. When you are sick, you seek health; when you are weak, you seek strength. Your desire for prosperity is the voice of God in you telling you that abundance is yours; therefore, through your poor state you find the urge to grow, to expand, to unfold, to achieve, and to accomplish your desires.

A pain in your shoulder is a blessing in disguise; it tells you to do something about it at once. If there were no pain and no indication of trouble, your arm might fall off on the street. Your pain is God's alarm system telling you to seek His Peace and His Healing Power, and to move from darkness to Light. When cold, you build a fire. When you are hungry, you eat. When you are in lack, enter into the mood of opulence and plenty. Imagine the end; rejoice in it. Having imagined the end and felt it as true, you have willed the means to the realization of the end.

When you are fearful and worried, feed your mind with the great truths of God that have stood the test of time and will last forever. You can receive comfort by meditating on the great Psalms. For example: "The Lord is my shepherd; I shall not want." "God is my refuge, my salvation, whom shall I fear?" "God is an ever-present help in time of trouble." "My God; in Him will I trust." "He shall cover me with His feathers, and under His wings shall I rest." "One with God is a majority." "If God be for me, who can be against me?" "I do all things through

Christ which strengtheneth me." Let the healing vibrations of these truths flood your mind and heart; then you will crowd out of your mind all your fears, doubts, and worries through this meditative process.

Imbibe another great spiritual truth: "A merry heart maketh a cheerful countenance." "A merry heart hath a continual feast." "A merry heart doeth good like a medicine; a broken spirit drieth the bones." "Therefore I put thee in remembrance that thou stir up the gift of God within thee." Begin *now* to stir up the gift of God by completely rejecting the evidence of senses, the tyranny and despotism of the race mind, and give complete recognition to the spiritual Power within you as the only Cause, the only Power, and the only Presence. Know that it is a responsive and beneficent Power. "Draw nigh unto It, and It will draw nigh unto you." Turn to It devotedly with assurance, trust, and love; It will respond to you as love, peace, guidance, and prosperity.

It will be your Comforter, Guide, Counselor, and your heavenly Father. You will then say, "God is Love. I have found Him, and He truly has delivered me from all my fears." Furthermore, you will find yourself in green pastures, where abundance and all of God's riches flow freely through you.

Say to yourself freely and joyously during the day, "I walk in the consciousness of the Presence of God all day long." "His fulness flows through me at all times, filling up all the empty vessels in my life."

When you are filled full of the feeling of being what you long to be, your prayer is answered. Are all the vessels full in your life? Look under health, wealth, love, and expression. Are you fully satisfied on all levels? Is there something lacking in one of these four? All that you seek, no matter what it is, comes under one of these classifications.

If you say, "All I want is truth or wisdom," you are expressing the desire of all men everywhere. That is what everyone wants, even though he or she may word it differently. Truth or wisdom is the overall desire of every man; this comes under the classification of expression. You wish to express more and more of God here and now.

Through your lack, limitation, and problems, you grow in God's Light, and you discover yourself. There is no other way whereby you could discover yourself.

If you could not use your powers two ways, you would never discover yourself; neither would you ever deduce a law governing you. If you were compelled to be good, or compelled to love, that would not be love. You would then be an automaton. You have freedom to love, because you can give it or retain it. If compelled to love, there is no love. Aren't you flattered when some woman tells you she loves you and wants you? She has chosen you from all the men in the world. She does not have to love you. If she were forced to love you, you would not be flattered or happy about it.

You have freedom to be a murderer or a holy man. That is the reason that we praise such men as Lincoln and others. They decided to choose the good; we praise them for their choice. If we believe that circumstances, conditions, events, age, race, religious training, or early environment can preclude the possibility of our attaining a happy, prosperous life, we are thieves and robbers. All that is necessary to express happiness and prosperity is to *feel* happy and prosperous. The feeling of wealth produces wealth. States of consciousness manifest themselves. This is why it is said, "All that ever came before me [feeling] are thieves and robbers." Feeling is the law, and the law is feeling.

Your desire for prosperity is really the promise of God saying that His riches are yours; accept this promise without any mental reservation.

Quimby likened prayer to a lawyer pleading the case before the judge. This teacher of the laws of mind said he could prove the defendant was not guilty as charged, but was instead a victim of lies and false beliefs. You are the judge: You render your own verdict; then you are set free. The negative thoughts of lack, poverty, and failure are all false; they are all lies; there is nothing to back them up.

You know there is only one spiritual Power, one primal cause, and you therefore cease giving power to conditions, circumstances, and opinions of men. Give all Power to the Spiritual Power within you, knowing that It will respond to your thought of abundance and prosperity. Recognizing the supremacy of the Spirit within, and the Power of your own thought or mental image, is the way to opulence, freedom, and constant supply. Accept the abundant life in your own mind. Your mental acceptance and expectancy of wealth has its own mathematics and mechanics of expression. As you enter into the mood of opulence, all things necessary for the abundant life will come to pass. You are now the judge arriving at a decision in the courthouse of your mind. You have, like Quimby, produced indisputable evidence showing how the laws of your mind work, and you are now free from fear. You have executed and chopped the heads off all the fear and superstitious thoughts in your mind. Fear is the signal for action; it is not really bad; it tells you to move to the opposite, which is faith in God and all positive values.

Let this be your daily prayer; write it in your heart: "God is the source of my supply. That supply is my supply now. His riches flow to me freely, copiously, and abundantly. I am forever conscious of my true worth. I give of my talents freely, and I am wonderfully, divinely compensated. Thank you, Father!"

THE ROAD TO RICHES

RICHES ARE OF the mind. Let us suppose for a moment that a physician's diploma were stolen together with his office equipment. I am sure you would agree that his wealth was in his mind. He could still carry on, diagnose disease, prescribe, operate, and lecture on materia medica. Only his symbols were stolen; he could always get additional supplies. His riches were in his mental capacity, knowledge to help others, and his ability to contribute to humanity in general.

You will always be wealthy when you have an intense desire to contribute to the good of mankind. Your urge for service—i.e. to give of your talents to the world—will always find a response in the heart of the universe.

I knew a man in New York during the financial crisis of 1929 who lost everything he had including his home and all his life's savings. I met him after a lecture which I had given at one of the hotels in the city. This was what he said: "I lost everything. I made a million dollars in four years. I will make it again. All I have lost is a symbol. I can again attract the symbol of wealth in the same way that honey attracts flies."

I followed the career of this man for several years to discover the key to his success. The key may seem strange to you; yet it is a very old one. The name he gave the key was, "Change water into wine!" He read this passage in the Bible, and he knew it was the answer to perfect health, happiness, peace of mind, and prosperity.

Wine in the Bible always means the realization of your desires, urges, plans, dreams, propositions, etc.; in other words, it is the things you wish to accomplish, achieve, and bring forth.

Water in the Bible usually refers to your mind or consciousness. Water takes the shape of any vessel into which it is poured; likewise, whatever you feel and believe as true will become manifest in your world; thus you are always changing water into wine.

The Bible was written by illumined men; it teaches practical, everyday psychology and a way of life. One of the cardinal tenets of the Bible is that you determine, mould, fashion, and shape your own destiny through right thought, feeling, and beliefs. It teaches you that you can solve any problem, overcome any situation, and that you are born to succeed, to win, and to triumph. In order to discover the Royal Road to Riches and receive the strength and security necessary to advance in life, you must cease viewing the Bible in the traditional way.

The above man who was in a financial crisis used to say to himself frequently during the days when he was without funds, "I can change water into wine!" These words meant to him, "I can exchange the poverty ideas in my mind for the realization of my present desires or needs which are wealth and financial supply."

His mental attitude (water) was, "Once I made a fortune honestly. I will make it again (wine)." His regular affirmation consisted of, "I attracted the symbol (money) once, I am attracting it again. I know this, and feel it is true (wine)."

This man went to work as a salesman for a chemical organization. Ideas for the better promotion of their products came to him; he passed them on to his organization. It was not long until he became vice president. Within four years the company made him president. His constant mental attitude was, "I can change water into wine!"

Look upon the story in John of changing water into wine in a figurative way, and say to yourself as this chemical salesman did: "I can make my invisible ideas, urges, dreams, and desires visible, because I have discovered a simple, universal law of mind."

The law he demonstrated is the law of action and reaction. It means your external world, body, circumstances, environment, and financial status are always a perfect reflection of your inner thinking, beliefs, feelings, and convictions. This being true, you can now change your inner pattern of thought by dwelling on the idea of success, wealth, and peace of mind. As you busy your mind with these latter concepts, these ideas will gradually seep into your mentality like seeds planted in the ground. As all seeds (thoughts and ideas) grow after their kind, so will your habitual thinking and feeling manifest in prosperity, success, and peace of mind. Wise thought (action) is followed by right action (reaction).

You can acquire riches when you become aware of the fact that prayer is a marriage feast. The *feast* is a psychological one; you meditate on (mentally eat of) your good or your desire until you become *one* with it.

I will now cite a case history from my files relating how a young woman performed her first miracle in transforming "water into wine." She operated a very beautiful hair salon. Her mother became ill, and she had to devote considerable time at home, neglecting her business. During her absence two of her assistants embezzled funds. She was forced into bankruptcy, lost her home, and found herself deeply in debt. She was unable to pay hospital bills for her mother, and she was now unemployed.

I explained to this woman the magic formula of changing water into wine. Again it was made clear to her that *wine* means answered prayer or the objectification of her ideal.

She was quarreling with the outside world. She said, "Look at the facts: I have lost everything; it is a cruel world. I cannot pay my bills. I do not pray, for I have lost hope." She was so absorbed and engrossed in the material world that she was completely unaware of the internal cause of her situation. As we talked, she began to understand that she had to resolve the quarrel in her mind.

No matter what your desire or ideal is as you read this book, you will also find some thought or idea in your mind opposed to it. For example, your desire may be for health; perhaps there are several thoughts such as these in your mind simultaneously: "I can't be healed. I have tried, but it is no use; it's getting worse." "I don't know enough about spiritual mind healing."

As you study yourself, don't you have a tug of war in your

mind? Like this girl, you find environment and external affairs challenging your desire of expression, wealth, and peace of mind.

True prayer is a mental marriage feast, and it teaches us all how to resolve the mental conflict. In prayer, you "write" what you *believe* in your own mind. Emerson said, "A man is what he thinks all day long." By your habitual thinking you make your own mental laws of belief. By repeating a certain train of thought you establish definite opinions and beliefs in the deeper mind called the subconscious; then such mental acceptances, beliefs, and opinions direct and control all the outer actions. To understand this and begin to apply it is the first step in changing "water into wine," or changing lack and limitation into abundance and opulence. The man who is unaware of his own inner spiritual powers is, therefore, subject to race beliefs, lack, and limitation.

Open your Bible now, and perform your first miracle, as this hairdresser did. You can do it. If you merely read the Bible as a historical event, you will miss the spiritual, mental, scientific view of the laws of mind with which we are concerned in this book.

Let us take this passage: "And the third day there was a marriage in Cana of Galilee; and the mother of Jesus was there." *Galilee* means your mind or consciousness. *Cana* means your desire. The *marriage* is purely mental, or the subjective embodiment of your desire. This whole beautiful drama of prayer is a psychological one in which all the characters are mental states, feelings, and ideas within you.

One of the meanings of *Jesus* is illumined reason. The *mother of Jesus* means the feeling, moods, or emotions which possess us.

"And both Jesus was called, and his disciples, to the marriage." Your *disciples* are your inner powers and faculties enabling you to realize your desires.

"And when they wanted wine, the mother of Jesus saith unto him, They have no wine." *Wine*, as we have stated, represents the answered prayer or the manifestation of your desire and ideals in life. You can now see this is an everyday drama taking place in your own life.

When you wish to accomplish something as this girl did—namely, finding work, supply, and a way out of your problem—suggestions of lack come to you, such as, "There is no hope. All is lost. I can't accomplish it; it is hopeless." This is the voice from the outside world saying to you, "They have no wine," or "Look at the facts." This is your feeling of lack, limitation, or bondage speaking.

How do you meet the challenge of circumstances and conditions? By now you are getting acquainted with the laws of mind, which are as follows: "As I think and feel inside, so is my outside world, i.e. my body, finances, environment, social position, and all phases of my external relationship to the world and man." Your internal, mental movements and imagery govern, control, and direct the external plane in your life.

The Bible says, "As he thinketh in his heart, so *is* he." The *heart* is a Chaldean word meaning the subconscious mind. In other words, your thought must reach subjective levels by engaging the power of your subliminal self.

Thought and feeling are your destiny. Thought charged with feeling and interest is always subjectified and becomes manifest in your world. *Prayer* is a marriage of thought and feeling, or your idea and emotion; this is what the marriage feast relates.

Any idea or desire of the mind felt as true comes to pass, whether it is good, bad, or indifferent. Knowing the law now—that what you imagine and feel in your mind, you will express, manifest, or experience in the outside—enables you to begin to discipline your mind.

When the suggestion of lack, fear, doubt, or despair ("they have no wine") comes to your mind, immediately reject it mentally by focussing your attention at once on the answered prayer, or the fulfillment of your desire.

The statements given in the Bible from John 2, "Mine hour is not yet come," and, "Woman, what have I to do with thee?" are figurative, idiomatic, Oriental expressions.

As we paraphrase these quotations, *woman* means the negative feeling that you indulge in. These negative suggestions have no power or reality, because there is nothing to back them up.

A suggestion of lack has no power; the power is resident in your own thought and feeling.

What does God mean to you? *God* is the name given to the One Spiritual Power. *God* is the One Invisible Source from which all things flow.

When your thoughts are constructive and harmonious, the Spiritual Power, being responsive to your thought, flows as harmony, health, and abundance. Practice the wonderful discipline of completely rejecting every thought of lack by immediately recognizing the availability of the Spiritual Power and Its response to your constructive thoughts and imagery; then you will be practicing the truth found in these words: "Woman, what have I to do with thee?"

We read, "Mine hour is not yet come." This means that while you have not yet reached a conviction or positive state of mind, you know you are on the way mentally, because you are engaging your mind on the positive ideals, goals, and objectives in life. Whatever the mind dwells upon, it multiplies, magnifies, and causes to grow until finally the mind becomes qualified with the new state of consciousness. You are then conditioned positively, whereas before you were conditioned negatively.

The spiritual man in prayer moves from the mood of lack to the mood of confidence, peace, and trust in the Spiritual Power within himself. Since his trust and faith are in the Spiritual Power, his mother (moods and feeling) registers a feeling of triumph or victory; this will bring about the solution or the answer to your prayer.

The waterpots in the story from the Bible refer to the mental cycles that man goes through in order to bring about the subjective realization of his desire. The length of time may be a moment, hour, week, or month, depending on the faith and state of consciousness of the student.

In prayer we must cleanse our mind of false beliefs, fear, doubt, and anxiety by becoming completely detached from the evidence of senses and the external world. In the peacefulness and quietude of your mind, wherein you have stilled the wheels of your mind, meditate on the joy of the answered prayer until that inner certitude comes whereby *you know that you know.* When you have succeeded in being *one* with your desire, you have succeeded in the mental marriage—or the union of your feeling with your idea.

I am sure you wish to be married to (one with) health, harmony, success, and achievement in your mind at this moment. Every time you pray you are trying to perform the *marriage feast of Cana* (realization of your desire or ideals). You want to be mentally identified with the concepts of peace, success, well-being, and perfect health.

"They filled them up to the brim." *The six waterpots* represent your own mind in the spiritual and mental creative act. You must fill your mind *to the brim*, meaning you must become filled full of the feeling of being what you long to be. When you succeed in filling your mind with the ideal you wish to accomplish or express, you are full to the brim; then you cease praying about it; for you feel its reality in your mind. You *know!* It is a finished state of consciousness. You are at peace about it.

"And he saith unto them, Draw out now, and bear unto the governor of the feast." Whatever is impregnated in our subconscious mind is always objectified on the screen of space; consequently, when we enter a state of conviction that our prayer is answered, we have given the command, "Bear unto the governor of the feast."

You are always governing your mental feast. During the day

thousands of thoughts, suggestions, opinions, sights, and sounds reach your eyes and ears. You can reject them as unfit for mental consumption or entertain them, as you choose. Your conscious, reasoning, intellectual mind is the governor of the feast. When you consciously choose to entertain, meditate, feast upon, and imagine your heart's desire as true, it becomes a living embodiment and a part of your mentality, so that your deeper self gives birth or expression to it. In other words, what is impressed subjectively is expressed objectively. Your senses or conscious mind see the objectification of your good. When the conscious mind becomes aware of "water made into wine," it becomes aware of the answered prayer. *Water* might also be called the invisible, formless, spiritual power, unconditioned consciousness. *Wine* is conditioned consciousness, or the mind giving birth to its beliefs and convictions.

The servants which draw the water for you represent the mood of peace, confidence, and faith. According to your faith or feeling, your good is attracted or drawn to you.

Imbibe, cherish, fall in love with these spiritual principles which are discussed in this book. In the first recorded miracle of Jesus, you are told that prayer is a marriage feast, or the mind uniting with its desire.

Love is the fulfilling of the law. Love is really an emotional attachment, a sense of oneness with your good. You must be true to that which you love. You must be loyal to your purpose or to your ideal. We are not being true to the one we love when we are flirting or mentally entertaining other marriages to fear, doubt, worry, anxiety, or false beliefs. Love is a state of oneness, a state of fulfillment. See *Love is Freedom*, p. 16.

When this simple drama was explained to the hairdresser mentioned above, she became rich mentally. She understood this drama, and she put it into practice in her life. This is how she prayed: She knew that the *water* (her own mind) would flow, and fill up all the *empty vessels* in response to her new way of thinking and feeling.

At night this client became very quiet and still, relaxed her body, and began to use constructive imagery. The steps she used are as follows:

The first step: She began to imagine that the local bank manager was congratulating her on her wonderful deposits in the bank. She kept imagining that for about five minutes.

The second step: In her imagination she heard her mother saying to her, "I am so happy about your wonderful, new position." She continued to hear her say this in a happy, joyous way for about three to five minutes.

The third step: She vividly imagined the writer was in front of her performing her marriage ceremony. This woman heard me saying as the officiating minister, "I now pronounce you man and wife." Completing this routine, she went off to sleep feeling filled full, i.e. sensing and feeling within herself the joy of the answered prayer.

Nothing happened for three weeks; in fact, things got much worse, but she persevered, refusing to take "No" for her answer. She knew that in order to grow spiritually, she, too, had to perform her first miracle by changing her fear to faith, her mood of lack to a mood of opulence and prosperity, by changing consciousness (water) into the conditions, circumstances, and experiences she wished to express.

Consciousness, Awareness, Beingness, Principle, Spirit, or whatever name you give It, is the cause of all; It is the only Presence and Power. The Spiritual Power or Spirit within us is the cause and substance of all things. All things—birds, trees, stars, sun, moon, earth, gold, silver, and platinum—are its manifestations. It is the cause and substance of all things. "There is none else."

Understanding this, she knew that *water* (consciousness)

could become supply in the form of money, true place, or true expression for herself, health for her mother, as well as companionship and fulness of life. She saw this simple—yet profound—truth in the twinkling of an eye, and she said to me, "I *accept my good.*"

She knew that nothing is hidden from us; all of God is within us, waiting for our discovery and inquiry.

In less than a month this young girl got married. The writer performed the ceremony. I pronounced the words she heard me say over and over again in her meditative, relaxed state, "I now pronounce you man and wife!"

Her husband gave her a check for $24,000 as a wedding present, as well as a trip around the world. Her new expression as a beauty-parlor operator was to beautify her home and garden and make the desert of her mind rejoice and blossom as the rose.

She "changed water into wine." *Water*, or her consciousness, became charged or conditioned by her constant, true, happy imagery. These images, when sustained regularly, systematically, and with faith in the developing powers of the deeper mind, will come out of the darkness (subconscious mind) into light (objectified on the screen of space).

There is one important rule: Do not expose this newly developed film to the shattering light of fear, doubt, despondency, and worry. Whenever worry or fear knocks at your door, immediately turn to the picture you developed in your mind, and say to yourself, "A beautiful picture is being developed now in the darkroom of my mind." Mentally pour on that picture your feeling of joy, faith, and understanding. You know you have operated a psychological, spiritual law; for what is impressed shall be expressed. It is wonderful!

The following is a sure, certain way for developing and manifesting all the material riches and supply you need all the days of your life. If you apply this formula sincerely and honestly, you should be amply rewarded on the external plane. I will illustrate this by telling you of a man who came to see me in London in desperate financial straits. He was a member of the Church of England and had studied the workings of the subconscious mind to some extent.

I told him to say frequently during the day, "God is the source of my supply, and all my needs are met at every moment of time and point of space." Think also of all the animal life in this world and of all the galaxies of space which are now being taken care of by an Infinite Intelligence. Notice how nature is lavish, extravagant, and bountiful. Think of the fish of the sea which are all being sustained, as well as the "birds of the air"!

He began to realize that since he was born, he had been taken care of, fed by his mother, clothed by his father, and watched over by tender, loving parents. This man got a job and was paid in a wonderful way. He reasoned that it was illogical to assume that the Principle of Life which gave him life and always took care of him would suddenly cease to respond to him.

He realized that he had cut off his own supply by resenting his employer, by self-condemnation, by criticism of himself, and by his own sense of unworthiness. He had psychologically severed the cord which joined him to the Infinite Source of all things—the Indwelling Spirit or Life Principle, called by some, "Consciousness or Awareness."

Man is not fed like the birds; he must consciously commune with the Indwelling Power and Presence and receive guidance, strength, vitality, and all things necessary for the fulfillment of his needs.

This is the formula which he used to change water into the wine of abundance and financial success. He realized God or the Spiritual Power within him was the cause of all; furthermore, he realized that if he could sell himself the idea that wealth was his by Divine right, he would manifest abundance of supply.

The affirmation he used was, "God is the source of my supply. All my financial and other needs are met at every moment of time and point of space; there is always a Divine surplus." This simple statement, repeated frequently, knowingly, and intelligently, conditioned his mind to a prosperity consciousness.

All he had to do was to sell himself this positive idea, in the same way that a good salesman has to sell himself on the merits of his product. Such a person is convinced of the integrity of his company, the high quality of the product, the good service which it will give the customer, and the fact that the price is right, etc.

I told him that whenever negative thoughts came to his mind, which would happen, not to fight or quarrel with them in any way, but simply go back to the spiritual, mental formula and repeat it quietly and lovingly to himself. At times negative thoughts came to him in avalanches and floods of negativity. Each time he met them with the positive, firm, loyal conviction: "God supplies all my needs; there is a Divine surplus in my life."

He said that as he drove his car and went through his day's routine, a host of sundry, miscellaneous, negative concepts crowded his mind from time to time, such as "There is no hope." "You are broke." Each time such negative thoughts came, he refused their mental admission by turning to the Eternal Source of wealth, health, and all things which he knew to be his own spiritual awareness. Definitely and positively he claimed, "God is the source of my supply, and that supply is mine now!" Or, "There is a Divine solution. God's wealth is my wealth," and other affirmative, positive statements which charged his mind with hope, faith, expectancy, and ultimately a conviction in an ever-flowing fountain of riches, supplying all his needs copiously, joyously, and endlessly.

The negative flood of thoughts came to him as often as fifty times an hour; each time he refused to open the door of his mind to these gangsters, assassins, and thieves which he knew would only rob him of peace, wealth, success, and all good things. Instead he opened the door of his mind to the idea of God's Eternal Life Principle of supply flowing through him as wealth, health, energy, power, and all things necessary to lead a full and happy life here.

As he continued to do this, on the second day not so many thieves knocked at his door; the third day, the flow of negative visitors was less; the fourth day, they came intermittently, hoping for admission, but receiving the same mental response: "No entrance! I accept only thoughts and concepts which activate, heal, bless, and inspire my mind!"

He reconditioned his consciousness or mind to a wealth consciousness. "The prince of this world cometh, and hath nothing in me." This means that the negative thoughts, such as fear, lack, worry, anxiety, came, but they received no response from his mind. He was now immune, God-intoxicated, and seized by a Divine faith in an ever-expanding consciousness of abundance and financial supply. This man did not lose everything; neither did he go into bankruptcy. He was given extended credit; his business improved; new doors opened up, and he prospered.

Remember always in the prayer process that you must be loyal to your ideal, purpose, and objective. Many people fail to realize wealth and financial success because they pray two ways. They affirm God is their supply and that they are Divinely prospered, but a few minutes later they deny their good by saying, "I can't pay this bill." "I can't afford this, that, or the other thing." Or they say to themselves, "A jinx is following me." "I can't ever make ends meet." "I never have enough to go around." All such statements are highly destructive and neutralize your positive prayers. This is what is called "praying two ways."

You must be faithful to your plan or your goal. You must be true to your knowledge of the Spiritual Power. Cease making negative marriages, i.e. uniting with negative thoughts, fears, and worries.

Prayer is like a captain directing the course of his ship. You must have a destination. You must know where you are going. The captain of the ship, knowing the laws of navigation, regulates his course accordingly. If the ship is turned from its course by storms or unruly waves, he calmly redirects it along its true course.

You are the captain on the bridge, and you are giving the orders in the way of thoughts, feelings, opinions, beliefs, moods, and mental tones. Keep your eye on the beam. *You go where your vision is!* Cease, therefore, looking at all the obstacles, delays, and impediments that would cause you to go off your course. Be definite and positive. Decide where you are going. Know that your mental attitude is the ship which will take you from the mood of lack and limitation to the mood and feeling of opulence, and to the belief in the inevitable law of God working for you.

Quimby, who was a wonderful student and teacher of the mental and spiritual laws of mind, said, "Man acts as he is acted upon." What moves you now? What is it that determines your response to life? The answer is as follows: Your ideas, beliefs, and opinions activate your mind and condition you to the point that you become, as Quimby stated, "An expression of your beliefs." This illustrates the truth of Quimby's statement: "Man is belief expressed."

Another popular statement of Quimby's was, "Our minds mingle like atmospheres, and each person has his identity in that atmosphere." When you were a child, you were subject to the moods, feelings, beliefs, and the general mental atmosphere of the home. The fears, anxieties, superstitions, as well as the religious faith and convictions of the parents were impressed on your mind.

Let us say the child had been brought up in a poverty-stricken home, in which there was never enough to go around, financially speaking; he heard constantly the complaint of lack and limitation.

You could say, like Salter in his conditioned-reflex therapy, that the child was conditioned to poverty. The young man may have a poverty complex based on his early experiences, training, and beliefs, but he can rise above any situation and become free; this is done through the power of prayer.

I knew a young boy, aged 17, who was born in a place called "Hell's Kitchen," in New York. He listened to some lectures I was giving in Steinway Hall, New York, at the time. This boy realized that he had been the victim of negative, destructive thinking, and that if he did not redirect his mind along constructive channels, the world mind with its fears, failures, hates, and jealousies would move in and control him. "Man acts as he is acted upon."

It stands to reason, as Quimby knew, that if man will not take charge of his own house (mind), the propaganda, false beliefs, fears, and worries of the phenomenalistic world will act as a hypnotic spell over him.

We are immersed in the race mind which believes in sickness, death, misfortune, accident, failures, disease, and diverse disasters. Follow the biblical injunction: "Come out from among them, and be separate." Identify yourself mentally and emotionally with the Eternal Verities which have stood the test of time.

This young man decided to think and plan for himself. He decided to take the Royal Road to Riches by accepting God's abundance here and now, and to fill his mind with spiritual concepts and perceptions. He knew that as he did this he would automatically crowd out of his mind all negative patterns.

He adopted a simple process called "scientific imagination." He had a wonderful voice, but it was not cultivated or developed. I told him the image he gave attention to in his mind would be developed in his deeper mind and come to pass. He understood this to be a law of mind—a law of action and reaction—i.e. the response of the deeper mind to the mental picture held in the conscious mind.

This young man would sit down quietly in his room at home, relax his whole body, and vividly imagine himself singing before a microphone. He would actually reach out for the "feel" of the instrument. He would hear me congratulate him on his wonderful contract and tell him how magnificent his voice was. By giving his attention and devotion to this mental image regularly and systematically, a deep impression was made on his subconscious mind.

A short time elapsed, and an Italian voice instructor in New York gave him free lessons several times a week, because he saw his possibilities. He got a contract which sent him abroad to sing in the salons of Europe, Asia, South Africa, and other places. His financial worries were over, for he also received a wonderful salary. His hidden talents and ability to release them were his real riches. These talents and powers within all of us are God-given; let us release them.

Did you ever say to yourself, "How can I be more useful to my fellow creatures?" "How can I contribute more to humanity?"

A minister-friend of mine told me that in his early days he and his church suffered financially. His technique or process was this simple prayer which worked wonders for him: "God reveals to me better ways to present the truths of God to my fellow creatures." Money poured in; the mortgage was paid in a few years, and he has never worried about money since.

As you read this chapter, you have now learned that the inner feelings, moods, and beliefs of man always control and govern his external world. The inner movements of the mind control the outer movements. To change the outside, you must change the inside. "As in Heaven, so on earth"; or, "As it is in my mind or consciousness, so is it in my body, circumstances, and environment."

The Bible says, "There is nothing hidden that shall not be revealed." For example, if you are sick, you are revealing a mental and emotional pattern which is the cause. If you are upset, or if you receive tragic news, notice how you reveal it in your face, eyes, gestures, tonal qualities, as well as your gait and posture. As a matter of fact, your whole body reveals your inner distress. You could, of course, through mental discipline and prayer remain absolutely poised, serene, and calm, refusing to betray your hidden feelings or mental states. You could order the muscles of your body to relax, be quiet, and be still; they would have to obey you. Your eyes, face, and lips would not betray any sign of grief, anger, or despondency. On the other hand, with a little discipline, through prayer and meditation you could reverse the entire picture. Even though you had received disturbing news, regardless of its grave nature you could show and exhibit joy, peace, relaxation, and a vibrant, buoyant nature. No one would ever know that you were the recipient of so-called bad news.

Regardless of what kind of news you received today, you could go to the mirror, look at your face, lips, eyes, and your gestures, as you tell yourself and imagine that you have heard the news of having received a vast fortune. Dramatize it, feel it, thrill to it, and notice how your whole body responds to the inner thrill.

You can reverse any situation through prayer. Busy your mind with the concepts of peace, success, wealth, and happiness. Identify yourself with these ideas mentally, emotionally, and pictorially.

Get a picture of yourself as you want to be; retain that image; sustain it with joy, faith, and expectancy; finally you will succeed in experiencing its manifestation.

I say to people who consult me regarding financial lack to

"marry wealth." Some see the point; others do not. As all Bible students know, your *wife* is what you are mentally joined to, united with, or at one with.

In other words, what you conceive and believe, you give conception to. If you believe the world is cold, cruel, and harsh—that it is a "dog eat dog" way of life—that is *your* concept; you are married to it, and you will have children or issue by that marriage. The children from such a mental marriage or belief will be your experiences, conditions, and circumstances, together with all other events in your life. All your experiences and reactions to life will be the image and likeness of the ideas which fathered them.

Look at the many wives the average man is living with, such as fear, doubt, anxiety, criticism, jealousy, and anger; these play havoc with his mind. Marry wealth by claiming, feeling, and believing: "God supplies all my needs according to his riches in glory." Or take the following statement and repeat it over and over again knowingly until your consciousness is conditioned by it or it becomes part of your meditation: "I am Divinely expressed, and I have a wonderful income." Do not say this in parrot-like fashion, but know that your train of thought is being engraved in your deeper mind, and it becomes a conditioned state of consciousness. Let the phrase become meaningful to you. Pour life, love, and feeling on it, making it alive.

One of my class students recently opened a restaurant. He phoned me, saying that he got married to a restaurant; he meant that he had made up his mind to be very successful, diligent, and persevering, and to see that his business prospered. This man's *wife* (mental) was his belief in the accomplishment of his desire or wish.

Identify yourself with your aim in life, and cease mental marriages with criticism, self-condemnation, anger, fear, and worry. Give attention to your chosen ideal, being full of faith and confidence in the inevitable law of prosperity and success.

You will accomplish nothing by loving your ideal one minute and denying it the next minute; this is like mixing acid and alkali—and you will get an inert substance. In going along the Royal Road to Riches, you must be faithful to your chosen ideal (your wife).

We find illustrations in the Bible relating to these same truths. For instance, "Eve came out of Adam's rib." *Your rib* is your concept, desire, idea, plan, goal, or aim in life.

Eve means the emotion, feeling nature, or the inner tone. In other words, you must mother the idea. The idea must be mothered, loved, and felt as true in order to manifest your aim in life.

The *idea* is the father; the *emotion* is the mother; this is the marriage feast which is always taking place in your mind.

Ouspensky spoke of the third element which entered in or was formed following the union of your desire and feeling. He called it the neutral element. We may call it "peace"; for God is Peace.

The Bible says, "And the government shall be on his shoulders." In other words, let Divine Wisdom be your guide. Let the subjective Wisdom within you lead, guide, and govern you in all your ways. Turn over your request to this Indwelling Presence, knowing in your heart and soul that it will dissipate the anxiety, heal the wound, and restore your soul to equanimity and tranquility. Open your mind and heart, and say, "God is my pilot. He leads me. He prospers me. He is my Counselor." Let your prayer be night and morning, "I am a channel through which God's riches flow ceaselessly, copiously, and freely." Write that prayer in your heart, inscribe it in your mind. Keep on the beam of God's glory!

The man who does not know the inner workings of his own mind is full of burdens, anxieties, and worries; he has not learned how to cast his burden on the Indwelling Presence and go free.

The Zen monk was asked by his disciple, "What is Truth?" He replied in a symbolic way by taking the bag off his back and placing it on the ground.

The disciple then asked him, "Master, how does it work?"

The Zen monk, still silent, placed the bag on his back, and walked on down the road singing to himself. The *bag* is your burden, or your problem. You cast it on the subjective Wisdom which knows all and has the "know how" of accomplishment. It knows only the answer.

Placing the bag again on his back means though I still have the problem, I now have mental rest and relief from the burden, because I have invoked the Divine Wisdom on my behalf; therefore I sing the song of triumph, knowing that the answer to my prayer is on the way, and I sing for the joy that is set before me. It is wonderful.

"Every man at the beginning doth set forth good wine; and when men have well drunk, then that which is worse; but thou hast kept the good wine until now." This is true of every man when he first enters a knowledge of the laws of the mind. He sets out with high spirits and ambitions. He is the new broom which sweeps clean, and he is full of good intentions; oftentimes he forgets the Source of power. He does not remain faithful to the Principle within him, which is scientific and effectual, that would lift him out of his negative experiences and set him on the high road to freedom and peace of mind. He begins to indulge mentally and emotionally in ideas and thoughts extraneous to his announced aim and goal. In other words, he is not faithful to his ideal or wife.

Know that the subjective or deeper self within you will accept your request, and being the great fabricator, it will bring it to pass in its own way. All you do is release your request with faith and confidence in the same way you would cast a seed in the ground, or mail a letter to a friend knowing the answer will come.

Did you ever go between two great rocks and listen to the echo of your voice? This is the way the Life Principle within you answers. *You* will hear the echo of your own voice. Your *voice* is your inner, mental movement of the mind—your inner, psychological journey where you feasted mentally on an idea until you were full; then you rested.

Knowing this law and how to use it, be sure you never become drunk with power, arrogance, pride, or conceit. Use the law to bless, heal, inspire, and lift up others, as well as yourself.

Man misuses the law by selfishly taking advantage of his fellow man; if you do, you hurt, and attract loss to, yourself. Power, security, and riches are not to be obtained externally. They come from the treasure-house of eternity within. We should realize that the *good wine* is always present, for God is the Eternal Now. Regardless of present circumstances, you can prove that your good is ever-present by detaching yourself mentally from the problem, going on the High Watch, and going about your Father's business.

To go on the High Watch is to envision your good, to dwell on the new concept of yourself, to become married to it and sustain the happy mood by remaining faithful—full of faith every step of the way—knowing that the wine of joy, the answered prayer, is on the way. "Now is the day of salvation." "The kingdom of heaven is at hand." "Thou hast kept the good wine until now."

You can—this moment—travel psychologically in your mind and enter mentally through Divine imagination into any desired state. The wealth, health, or invention you wish to introduce are all invisible at first. Everything comes out of the Invisible. You must subjectively possess riches before you can objectively possess wealth. The feeling of wealth produces wealth; for wealth is a state of consciousness. *A state of consciousness* is what you think, feel, believe, and mentally give consent to.

A teacher in California receiving over five or six thousand dollars a year looked in a window at a beautiful ermine coat that was priced at $8,000. She said, "It would take me years to save that amount of money. I could never afford it. Oh, how I want it!" She listened to our lectures on Sunday mornings. By ceasing to marry these negative concepts, she learned that she could have a coat, a car, or anything she wished without hurting anybody on the face of the earth.

I told her to imagine she had the coat on, to feel its beautiful fur, and to get the feel of it on her. She began to use the power of her imagination prior to sleep at night. She put on the imaginary coat and fondled and caressed it, like a child with her doll. She continued to do this and finally felt the thrill of it all.

She went to sleep every night wearing this imaginary coat and being so happy in possessing it. Three months went by and nothing happened. She was about to waver, but she reminded herself that it is the sustained mood which demonstrates. "He who perseveres to the end shall be saved." The solution will come to the person who does not waver but always goes about with the perfume of His Presence with him. The answer comes to the man who walks in the light that "It is done!" You are always using the *perfume of His Presence* when you sustain the happy, joyous mood of expectancy, knowing your good is on the way. You saw it in the unseen, and you *know* you will see it in the seen.

The sequel to the teacher's drama of the mind is interesting. One Sunday morning after our lecture, a man accidentally stepped on her toe, apologized profusely, asked her where she lived, and offered to drive her home. She accepted gladly. Shortly after, he proposed marriage, gave her a beautiful diamond ring, and said to her, "I saw the most wonderful coat; you would look simply radiant wearing it!" It was the coat she had admired three months previously. (The salesman said over one hundred wealthy women looked at the coat, admired it immensely, but for some reason always selected another garment.)

Through your capacity to choose, imagine the reality of what you have selected, and through faith and perseverance *you can* realize your goal in life. All the riches of heaven are here now within you, waiting to be released. Peace, joy, love, guidance, inspiration, goodwill, and abundance all exist now. All that is necessary in order to express God's riches is for you to leave the present now (your limitation), enter into the mental vision or picture, and in a happy, joyous mood become one with your ideal. Having seen and felt your good in moments of high exaltation, you know that in a little while you shall see your ideal objectively as you walk through time and space. As within, so without. As above, so below. As in heaven, so on earth. In other words, you will see your beliefs expressed. Man *is* belief expressed!

The Healing
Power of Love

ONE OF THE most beautiful, soul-stirring stories in the Bible is the loving, moving account of Ruth and Boaz. *Ruth* means that which lovingly clings. *Boaz* means God's Truth. These are the two pillars which lead to the Holy of Holies within you.

You love God when you steadfastly refuse to give power to error and false beliefs, at the same time giving all your allegiance and devotion to the Spiritual Principle within you, insisting that the Principle of Harmony be manifested in your life. When you mentally reject the power of the phenomenal world and give all your allegiance to the Spirit within as Omnipotent, knowing It is responsive to your thought, you have the Lord of Life as your shepherd and you are loving God because you are being loyal to the One Power.

Ruth said to her mother-in-law, Naomi, "Intreat me not to leave thee, or to return from following after thee: for whither thou goest, I will go; and where thou lodgest, I will lodge: thy people shall be my people, and thy God my God" (Ruth 1:16).

Naomi is the emotional self. The Bible says her two sons are dead, which means that the body and environment are expressing lack and limitation. When you are not manifesting or expressing the desires of your heart, you become frustrated and disappointed. This is a story about all of us. A woman's husband is dead, biblically speaking, when the action of God has ceased to be expressed through her. She is no longer being impregnated by Divine Ideas such as Goodness, Truth, and Beauty. To put this in simple, psychological language, the emotions of defeat and despair are governing the consciousness. When a person lacks faith and confidence, and when initiative and the forward push are absent, truly the husband is dead. The woman in all of us is our emotional or subjective nature. Thought is the husband, and feeling is the woman.

"Thy maker is thy husband." The male quality of the mind is your husband which means thought, action, desire, or the image-making faculty. When you are functioning spiritually, you desire to grow, expand, and move forward. Life is a progression. When the mind is sick and confused, the emotions are disturbed; in such a case the tendency is to withdraw within yourself and brood; then your ideas, dreams, and aspirations die within you, and you feel frustrated. Your present state of consciousness and your desire are your two sons. If you are healthy, happy, joyous, and prosperous, your two sons are alive. If you are full of fear and foreboding, and wallowing in the mire of despair and despondency, your two sons are dead. Naomi (mother-in-law, the emotional nature) may be full of despair; yet the spiritual urge within all of us pushes us to move on, to press on up higher. It is the Voice of God crying in the wilderness, saying to all men, "Make straight in the desert a highway for our God" (Isaiah 40:2).

Ruth represents that which lovingly clings to us. It is the Cosmic Urge, the Divine Impulse in all of us. It clings to us, haunts our minds, and is a persistent voice insisting upon our attention. Life is always seeking to express itself.

"Whither shall I go from thy spirit? or whither shall I flee from thy presence?" (Psalm 139:7). The Presence of God is in the sick man, in the man whose body is racked with pain. "Behold, I am there." There is something within man which reminds him of his origin and urges him back to it. It is his mission and purpose to cherish, enlarge, and liberate this memory so that it grows from a spark to a flame and floods his whole being.

Ruth is called the female companion. She represents the unconscious desire of life to express itself and preserve itself at all costs. This inner female companion, or God in you, acts as a stimulus to your depressed state, causing you to think and reason a way out of your dilemma. She could be called the mother in you, or the intuitive sense in you. All men want to be good, do good, and express good because their nature is divine. God is in all men seeking to express Himself through them. Every man is an incarnation of God, and when you have a desire to be greater than you are, it is God seeking to express that concept or urge through you. Relax, let go, adopt the mood of receptivity, and let God's fullness flow through you. "There is a Divinity Which shapes our ends, rough hew them how we will."

Note carefully what Ruth in you says: "Whither thou goest, I will go; and where thou lodgest, I will lodge: thy people shall be my people, and thy God my God." For tender beauty, this statement is unsurpassed. Here is portrayed love, faith, and devotion to the end. "Where thou diest, I will die, and there will I be buried." Your faith in your ideal or goal must be maintained unto the end; then the old state dies and the new state (answered prayer) is resurrected. Ruth is really Life's urge seeking expression and progression through you. The journey is ever onward in consciousness. Ruth's urge in you is your love for God and all things spiritual. Fall in love with Wisdom, Truth, and Beauty, and wonders will take place in your life.

Boaz is the goal, the ideal you seek in life. You must have a goal in life, an aim, a purpose. You must be going somewhere, otherwise you simply drift aimlessly. Listen to Ruth, the inner promptings and murmurings of your heartstrings. If you do not know what your true place in life is, pray for guidance, and you will get a lead such as a strong, persistent feeling or tendency in a certain direction. An idea may suddenly come to your mind just as toast pops out of a toaster. The desire that lingers week in and week out is the true desire of your heart.

A boy of sixteen who recently prayed for guidance, for true expression in life, found himself joining religious groups, studying religious books, being interested in the Bible, etc. He plans to go to divinity school and is very happy about it. Later on he will teach the laws of life and the way of the Spirit to all men. He prayed for guidance, so the deeper mind responded accordingly. If a certain premise is enthroned in the mind, the response must be the correlate of the premise. The premise and conclusion are one; the beginning and the end are the same; the seed and the plant are one. He had invoked the spirit of guidance, and having once invoked it and believed in it, he came under the spell of right action.

I talked to a man who was offered a position overseas. He could not accept because of his intense fear of water and airplanes. He became panic-stricken at the thought of getting on a boat. Undoubtedly there was a subconscious pattern behind this, a terrifying childhood experience, perhaps at the hands of some bully in the neighborhood pool. He had prayed for true expression, his prayer had been answered, but he said he could not accept.

There is a way to overcome such fear. Ruth is the predominant part of the soul in man, telling him there is always a way out, a solution. The mere fact that he came to see me regarding help for his problem showed that he knew instinctively there was a way to overcome this fear. He was recognizing a Higher Power than his intellect.

He began to use his imagination constructively. He imagined and felt himself swimming in a pool, he felt the chill of the water, he made it vivid, real, and dramatic. He heard friends congratulate him on his progress. He became thoroughly immersed in the water mentally; it was a victorious, loving, interested movement of the mind.

He entered the water mentally until he was compelled to enter it physically. With the help of an instructor, he learned to swim and mastered the water. This was the working of the Spiritual Power which he invoked. The Spiritual Power responded according to the nature of his invocation or prayer and compelled him to respond; such is the law.

What we do on the inside, we experience on the outside. The Bible says, "Acquaint now thyself with Him, and be at peace, therefore good shall come to thee." Acquaint yourself with the mental and emotional operations of your own mind. Apply the principle of mind, realize your desire, and peace shall come unto thee.

Boaz means the Power and Wisdom of God. Boaz is that which blesses, heals, and makes you happy; Ruth (inner guidance) will lead you to it. It might be an invention you wish accepted, a desire to achieve in some field such as that of a singer, composer, great artist, or musician. Boaz is that which you wish to unite with in consciousness. You must marry Boaz. How do you marry or become one with your ideal (Boaz)? "Wash thyself therefore, and anoint thee, and put thy raiment upon thee" (Ruth 3:3).

Your good is your God. *Wash thyself* means to cleanse your mind by refusing to give power to anything but your own consciousness and the reigning power of your thought. Refuse positively and definitely to let your mind dwell on any negative state. To lift up your ideal is the meaning of *anoint thyself*. Look to your ideal, let the light shine on it, honor it, count it worthy, praise it, exalt it, tell yourself how wonderful your ideal is, and mentally accept it. Let your ideal captivate and enthrall you (wearing the garment). You will find a deific response within you. The Power or Principle within responds to your dominant thought and mood. It is called in modern science the law of action and reaction. You must fulfill certain conditions. There is something you must do before there is a divine response. Isaiah says, "Ask me of things to come concerning my sons, and concerning the works of my hand, command ye me."

God works through you, through your own thought and belief. In order for you to advance and grow spiritually, you must begin; then God begins. God will do nothing for you except through you. God works, of course, on a cosmic, universal scale in the control of all your vital functions and other body processes; beyond that you must initiate further growth and spiritual unfoldment. You must individualize and personalize the spirit in you.

The greatest study of man is man. This seems to be forgotten in our world today where we are feverishly engaged in building new hydrogen bombs. We must go back to God from whence we came. "So Boaz took Ruth, and she was his wife; and when he went in unto her, the Lord gave her conception, and she bare a son" (Ruth 4:13). That son was to be the father of Jesse and the grandfather of David. When you come to God, to Truth, and to the Eternal Source, realizing the Source is Love, there is no fear—only peace.

Begin now to meditate, to eat of the nourishing Truths of God which have stood the test of time. Feast on God's Love, Peace, Joy, Bliss, Beauty, and Perfection. Your mind will be nourished. Your soul will be fortified. God and His Peace will move on the waters of your mind. You will then be Ruth marrying Boaz, and you will give birth to a mental and spiritual child. He will be the father of the line of Jesse and David, meaning that you will experience the joy of the answered prayer—peace, health, and happiness.

Jesse means I AM or God, and *David* means Love. Your sense of union with God will be the progenitor or father of all things good in your world. Jesse (I AM), the awareness of the Presence of God, is born in your mind, and David, which is God's Love, rules your heart. You will have found your saviour, your companion, your guide, your loving friend who will remain with you always. You will have arrived at the state of consciousness called Ruth when your human love is raised to Divine Love by detaching yourself from the false beliefs of the world, and by giving all your devotion and attention to the real spiritual values of life. In other words, you will be functioning as Ruth and Boaz by following always where Divine Love leads and remaining steadfast in your belief and loyalty to the One Power.

Love in the highest and best degree, and acknowledge the God of Love as Lord of your life. Such loyalty and devotion are always rewarded, and you will find yourself a ruler of your world full of joy, happiness, and peace. You will go from glory to glory, ever onward, upward, and Godward.

Why Did This Happen To Me?

Remember ye not the former things, neither consider the things of old.

—Isaiah 43:18

But this one thing I do, forgetting those things which are behind, and reaching forth unto those things which are before, I press toward the mark for the prize. . . .

—Phil. 3:13, 14

Whatsoever a man soweth, so also shall he reap. This means that if we plant thoughts of peace, harmony, health, and prosperity, we shall reap accordingly; and that if we sow thoughts of sickness, lack, strife, and contention, we shall reap these things. We must remember that our subconscious mind is like the soil; it will grow whatever type of seed we plant in the garden of our mind. We sow thoughts, biblically speaking, when we believe them wholeheartedly, and it is what we really believe deep down in our hearts that we demonstrate.

113

I had a friend who was bedridden with disease, and during my visit to her at a hospital in London, she said to me, "Why did this happen to me? What did I do to deserve this? Why is God angry at me? Why is God punishing me?" Her friends pointed out to me how kindhearted and deeply spiritual she was, and that she was a pillar of the church, etc.

It is true that she was an excellent person in many ways, but she believed in the reality of her sickness and that the condition was incurable. She believed that her heart was governed by laws of its own, independent of her thinking. This was her belief, so naturally she demonstrated accordingly. She changed her belief and began to realize that her body was spiritual and that when she changed her mind, she changed her body. She began to cease giving power to the sickness in her thought and prayed as follows: "The Infinite Healing Presence is flowing through me as harmony, health, peace, wholeness, and perfection. God's Healing Love indwells every cell." She repeated this prayer frequently, and following her change of belief she had a wonderful healing. This woman had lived in fear of a heart attack for several years, not knowing that what we fear most comes to pass.

The law of life is the law of belief. Trouble of any kind is Nature's alarm signal that we are thinking wrongly in that direction, and nothing but a change of thought can set us free. Man is belief expressed, said Quimby, and we demonstrate what we really believe. There is a law of cause and effect operating at all times, and nothing happens to man without his mental consent and participation. You do not have to think of an accident to have it befall you.

Dr. Paul Tournier, the famous French psychiatrist, writes about a man who cut his hand with a saw and blamed the so-called accident on the fact that the wood which he was cutting was very wet. Dr. Tournier knew that there was a mental and emotional cause behind the severe cut on the man's hand. He discovered that the man was very irritated toward his employer, and that furthermore he had considerable rancor and hostility toward a former employer who had discharged him. Dr. Tournier explained to the man that when he is irritated and upset emotionally, his efforts become uncoordinated and jerky, and thus the accident had happened.

In the thirteenth chapter of Luke we read the following:

There were present at that season some that told him of the Galilaeans, whose blood Pilate had mingled with their sacrifices. And Jesus answering said unto them, Suppose ye that these Galilaeans were sinners above all the Galilaeans, because they suffered such things? I tell you, Nay, but except ye repent, ye shall all likewise perish. Or those eighteen, upon whom the tower in Siloam fell, and slew them, think ye that they were sinners above all men that dwelt in Jerusalem? I tell you, Nay, but, except ye repent, ye shall all likewise perish.

Jesus denies categorically that the victims of such calamities are worse sinners than other men, and adds *Except ye repent, ye shall likewise perish.* Misfortune, accidents, and tragedies of various kinds are signs of mental and emotional disorders that have broken out into manifestation. To repent means to think in a new way, to turn back to God and align our thoughts and mental imagery with the Infinite Life, Love, Truth, and Beauty of God, and then we become channels for the Divine.

Still your mind several times a day and affirm slowly, quietly, and lovingly, "God flows through me as harmony, health, peace, joy, wholeness, and perfection. God walks and talks in me. God's spell is always around me, and wherever I go God's Wisdom governs me in all my ways, and Divine right action prevails. All my ways are ways of pleasantness, and all my paths are peace."

As you dwell on these eternal verities, you will establish patterns of Divine Order in your subconscious mind; and since whatever you impress is expressed, you will find yourself watched over at all times by an Overshadowing Presence, your Heavenly Father, who responds to you when you call upon Him.

All of us are in the race mind, the great psychic sea of life. The race mind believes in sickness, accidents, death, misfortune, and tragedies of all kinds, and if we do not repent, i.e. if we do not do our own thinking, the race mind will do our thinking for us. Gradually the thoughts of the race mind impinging on our consciousness may reach a point of saturation and precipitate an accident, sudden illness, or calamity. The majority of people do not think; they *think* they think. You are thinking when you differentiate between that which is false and that which is true. To think is to choose. You have the capacity to say yes and no. Say *yes* to the Truth and reject everything unlike God or the Truth. If the mental instrument could not choose, you would not be an individual. You have the ability to accept and reject. *Think on whatsoever things are lovely, whatsoever things are just, whatsoever things are honest, whatsoever things are pure . . . think on these things.*

You are thinking when you know that there is an Infinite Intelligence which responds to your thoughts, and that no matter what the problem is, as you think about a Divine solution and the happy ending, you will find a subjective wisdom within you responding to you, revealing the perfect plan, and showing you the way you should go.

Some months ago a woman visited me stating that she had had an organic lesion for several years which failed to heal. She had taken all kinds of therapy including X-ray. She had prayed and sought prayer therapy from others without results. She told me, "God has it in for me. I'm a sinner, and this is why I am being punished." She also told me that she went to a man who hypnotized her, read her past, and had the effrontery and the audacity to tell her that she was a victim of karma, that she had wounded people in a former life, punishing them unjustly, and that now she was suffering and reaping her just deserts. Poignantly she asked, "Do you think this is why I can't be healed?"

All this is so much folderol and a monstrous absurdity. The above explanation compounded the misery and pain of the woman and offered no cure or solace. I explained to her an age-old Truth: that there is but one Power called God. It is the Creative Intelligence in all of us which created us. This Power becomes to us what we believe It to be. If a person thinks that God is punishing him and that he must suffer, *according to his thought and belief is it done unto him. As a man thinketh in his heart so is he.* This means that man's thoughts and feelings create his destiny. Man is what he thinks all day long, and if a man fails to think constructively, wisely, and judiciously, then someone else or the race mind will do his thinking for him and perhaps make a complete mess of his life.

If you believe that God is Infinite Goodness, Boundless Love, Absolute Harmony, and Boundless Wisdom, the God-Presence will respond accordingly by the law of reciprocal relationship, and you will find yourself blessed in countless ways. The forces of life are not evil; it depends how we use them. Atomic energy is not evil; it is good or bad depending on the way we use it. Man can use electricity to kill another or to vacuum the floor. You can use water to quench a child's thirst or to drown it. The wind which blows the ship on the rocks can also carry it to safety. The uses to which all things or objects in the world are put are determined by the thought of man. It is the mind of man which determines the use of the forces and objects in the world. Good and evil are movements in the mind of man relative to the One Power, which is whole, pure, and perfect. The Creative Force is in man. There is no power in the manifest universe except we give power to externals. This woman was seeking justification and alibis for her suffering. She was looking outside herself instead of realizing that the cause is always in her subconscious mind.

I asked her to tell me about her relationship with men. She confessed that she had an illicit love affair five years previously and that she felt guilty and full of remorse. This unresolved remorse was the psychic wound behind her organic lesion. She realized that God was not punishing her, but she was punishing herself by her own thoughts. The lesion was solidified thought which she could unthink. Life or God does not punish. If you burn your finger, Life proceeds to reduce the edema, gives you new skin, and restores it to wholeness. If you eat some tainted food, Life causes you to regurgitate and seeks to restore you to perfect health. The ancients said that the doctor dresses the wound, and God heals it.

The lesion and the morbid symptoms that no medical treatment or prayer therapy could heal, or had been able to cure, disappeared in a week. There is no worse suffering than a guilty conscience and certainly none more destructive. This woman had been punishing herself for five years by her destructive thinking, and when she ceased to condemn herself and began to claim that the Infinite Healing Presence was saturating her whole being and that God indwelled every cell of her body, the lesion disappeared. If you had been misusing the principle of electricity or chemistry for fifty years and you suddenly used it correctly, surely you would not say that the principle of electricity had a grudge against you because you had misused it. Likewise, no matter how long you may have used your mind in a negative and destructive manner, the minute you begin to use it the right way, right results follow. *Remember not the former things, neither consider the things of old* (Isaiah 43:18).

A man who came to see me some months ago was gradually losing his vision. He was attributing it to lack of vitamins, heredity factors, and pointed out that his grandfather went blind at eighty years of age. He belonged to a strange cult, and the cult leader, after reading his horoscope, said the planets were in a malefic configuration and that this was the cause of his failing vision. It is well known in psychosomatic circles today that psychic factors play a definite role in all disease. Nearsightedness can be brought on by workings of the mind. Treating the mental and emotional factors of the individual rather than the eye may reveal the basic emotional factor, the reason why the subconscious mind is selecting an ailment which tends to shut out everything except the immediate surroundings.

Dr. Flanders Dunbar states that certain emotional reactions can cause the involuntary muscles to twist the eyeball out of shape. In talking to this man, he revealed that he hated the sight of his mother-in-law who was living in his home. He was full of suppressed rage, and his emotional system which could not stand the strain any longer selected the eyes as the scapegoat. The explanation was the cure in this case. He was surprised to learn that negative emotions, if persisted in, snarl up in the subconscious mind and, being negative, must have a negative outlet. The negative commands to his subconscious mind—"I hate the sight of her," "I don't want to see her anymore"—were accepted by the deeper mind as a request which brought it to pass.

He made arrangements for his mother-in-law to live elsewhere and prayed for her by releasing her to God and wishing for her all the blessings of Heaven. His vision began to improve almost immediately, and in two weeks his eyesight was restored to normal. He knew he had forgiven his mother-in-law because he could meet her in his mind, and there was no longer any sting. He was trying to justify his failing vision by explaining it in terms of outside causes rather than his own mind.

A deficiency of Vitamin A can cause ophthalmia, which is an inflammation of the conjunctiva or of the eyeball; nevertheless, this could be due to ignorance, indifference, or negligence on the part of the individual. The cause in this case would be stupidity or carelessness, and the latter is a state of mind or simply a lack of knowledge. Vitamin A is omnipresent and we should have the intelligence to use it.

You cannot dodge or circumvent the law of mind. It is done unto you as you believe, and a belief is a thought in the mind. No external power or evil entity is trying to lure or harm you. People are constantly attributing their ailments to the atmosphere, the weather, to malpractice, evil entities, germs, viruses, and diet. Man pollutes the air with his strange notions and false doctrines. If a man believes that by being near an electric fan he will catch cold or get a stiff neck, that belief when accepted by him becomes his master and ruler and causes him to experience a cold. This is why the Bible says, *According to your faith is it done unto you.* The fan has no power to give anyone a stiff neck; it is harmless. Your faith can be used two ways. You can have faith in an invisible virus to give you the flu, or you can have faith in the Invisible Spirit within you to flow through you as harmony, health, and peace.

Realize that God cannot be sick, and that the Spirit in you is God; what is true of God is true of you. Believe this and you will never be sick, for *according to your faith* (in health and happiness) *is it done unto you.* Emerson said, "He [man] thinks his fate alien because the copula is hidden. But the soul contains the event that shall befall it; for the event is only the actualization of its thoughts, and what we pray to ourselves for is always granted. The event is the print of your form. It fits you like your skin" (from Emerson's essay "Fate").

The Devil in the Bible means ignorance or misunderstanding. Spell *live* backward and you have *evil.* Your evil is an inversion of the Life-Principle, which is God. God moves as a unity and seeks to express Himself through you as beauty, love, joy, peace, and Divine Order. The false idea in your mind is called the adversary, devil, Satan, etc. The devils which bedevil man are enmity, strife, hatred, revenge, hostility, self-condemnation, and other negative emotions. If man fails to believe in the goodness of God and in a God of Love, the extent to which he disbelieves can well be his so-called devil, which is the source of his pains, aches, and misfortunes.

A woman wrote me stating that her daughter was watching a group of men fighting on the streets of New York and that a bullet hit her daughter, necessitating the amputation of two fingers—and what was the cause of it? Was it God's will? Was it punishment for her sins that the accident occurred? The answer is in the negative to all these questions of the mother. God does not judge or punish; good and evil are the movements of man's own mind. It is very primitive thinking to believe that God is punishing us or that a devil is tempting us. Our state of consciousness is always made manifest. Men, women, and children are constantly testifying to our state of consciousness. Our state of consciousness is always cause.

We do not know the contents of this girl's mind. If she was hateful, resentful, or full of hostility and self-condemnation, she could have attracted such a condition to herself. We must remember that the majority of people do not discipline, control, or direct their thinking and mental imagery along God-like channels; therefore, their failure to think constructively and harmoniously from the standpoint of the Infinite One means that they leave their minds open to the irrational mass mind, which is full of fears, hates, jealousies, and all kinds of negative happenings.

Man's failure to think the right way is as bad as thinking negatively and destructively. I remember a farmer in Ireland who waited behind a fence every day for over a week in order to shoot the landlord when he passed by. One day he was going behind the usual fence, when he stumbled, the rifle went off, and he was shot fatally. I did not understand the reason at that time, and like others, I believed it to be an accident. There are no accidents; there is a mind, a mood, a feeling behind that car, train, bicycle, and also behind the gun. This man had murder in his heart for a long time, and his subconscious responded accordingly.

No manifestation cometh unto me, save I the Father draw it. The father is your state of consciousness, your own creative power, and no experience comes to you except there is an affinity in your own mind. Two unlike things repel each other. If you walk and talk with God and believe that God is guiding you and that the Law of Harmony is always governing you, then you cannot be on a train that is wrecked because discord and harmony do not dwell together. The mother added in her letter as a postscript, "My daughter cannot get her fingers back through prayer." I don't know why people are so determined and categorical in their statements that a man cannot grow a leg or finger if missing.

Let me quote from *He Heals To-Day*, by Elsie Salmon: "Mildred was three years old when brought to me. She was born without a left hand. The arm ended in a point no bigger than the size of an index finger well above the wrist. Within a month the point at the end of the deformed arm had doubled in size and was quite plump, whereupon the father, now seeing this remarkable development, said, 'Anything can happen.' The following month there was a formation which looked like a thumb and which, at the time, we thought was a thumb. About three months following we found that this was not a thumb at all but that the growth was the whole hand at the end of the arm, and this was unfolding like a flower before our eyes."

She concludes by saying that those who were skeptical are now accepting it as an established fact. Perhaps we should take a lesson from the rhinoceros. When you take off his horns and cut out the roots, he grows new horns. Cut the legs off a crab, and he grows new legs. If a man believed he could grow a new finger, leg, or any organ, he could experience his belief.

Let us cease blaming others; let us look within for the cause of all. Believe in God, in the goodness of God, in the love of God, and in God's guidance, and you will find that all your ways will be those of pleasantness, and all your paths will be paths of peace. You are belief expressed.

Magic of Faith

THE PURPOSE OF THIS essay is to reveal to you the spiritual truth of your dominion and freedom. *In all thy ways acknowledge him, and he shall direct thy paths* (Proverbs 3:6). *I will lift up mine eyes unto the hills, from whence cometh my help* (Psalm 121:1).

In the above verse from Proverbs you are told to acknowledge the Infinite Intelligence within you and that It shall direct you in all ways. The answer to your problem will come when you turn in faith and recognition to the Divine Principle within.

It was Shakespeare who said, "Our doubts are traitors, making us lose the good we oft might win, by fearing to attempt." Fear holds us back. *Fear* is a lack of faith in God or the Good.

A man once told me that he was a member of a sales force for a large chemical organization which had two hundred men in the field. The sales manager died, and the vice president offered him the position; however, he turned it down. He realized later that the only reason he had rejected the offer was one of fear. He had been afraid to assume the responsibility. This man lacked faith in himself and his Inner Power. He hesitated, and the wonderful opportunity passed him by.

This salesman came to me for consultation, and I learned he was condemning himself, which was like a destructive, mental poison. I made him aware of this, and in place of condemnation, he began to realize there were other opportunities. I explained to him that faith is a way of thinking, a positive mental attitude, or a feeling of confidence that what you are praying for will come to pass. He thereupon began to affirm boldly: "God is guiding me and reveals my true place to me." He was led to a new and wonderful position. He constantly exalts God in the midst of him.

For example, you have faith that the sun will rise tomorrow. You have faith that the seed you deposited in the ground will grow. The electrician has faith that electricity will respond to his proper use of it. A scientist has an idea for a computer; he proceeds to bring it to pass by having faith in the execution of the invisible idea.

Opportunity is always knocking at your door. The desire for health, harmony, peace, and prosperity is knocking at your door now. Perhaps you are offered a promotion; are you going to act like Peter of old who walked on the water? *And when Peter was come down out of the ship, he walked on the water, to go to Jesus. But when he saw the wind boisterous, he was afraid; and beginning to sink, he cried, saying, Lord, save me* (Matthew 14:29, 30).

Besides being historically true, this drama of Peter and Jesus takes place in your own mind. *Peter* means faith, perseverance, and determination. *Jesus* means your desire which, if realized, would be your saviour. Jesus comes into your mind as an idea, desire, plan, purpose, vision, or some new undertaking. The realization of your dreams, plans, or purpose would bring you and others great satisfaction and inner joy: this would be your Jesus. You must now call Peter, which is faith in the God-Power, to bring all things to pass. Look at Peter and Jesus as dramatizations of the power of truth within you.

Oftentimes as you attempt something new—for example, accepting a position—doubt comes into your mind; this is *Peter* in you looking at the *boisterous wind and sinking.* This represents the impingement in your mind of the race belief in failure, lack, and limitation.

You must cremate, burn up, and otherwise destroy that negative thought immediately. You must not suffer a witch to live, meaning you must supplant the negative feeling with the positive thoughts of success, peace, and prosperity immediately, and give your love and feeling to these concepts. As you sustain this mood of confidence, you will become victorious.

Doubt and fear hold men in bondage of sickness and failure. These false concepts cause you to vacillate, waver, equivocate, and hesitate to go ahead. The way to overcome this negative attitude is to increase your faith and awareness of your deep, spiritual potencies. Be like Peter; he succeeded because he went forward; he had faith and confidence, knowing he would succeed.

A general in charge of his troops cannot afford to vacillate and waver on the battlefield. He has to come to a decision. Otherwise defeat is inevitable. Failure to come to a decision, plus a constant wavering in the mind, leads to a nervous breakdown and mental confusion in the everyday world. When you find yourself being pulled two ways, that is a sign of doubt and fear.

Your good comes to you in the form of your desire. If you are sick, you wish health. If you are poor, you desire wealth. If you are full of fear, you desire faith and confidence. Jesus comes as your desire walking down the streets of your mind.

There is another part of your mind which says, "No, it can't be. It is too late now." "It is impossible." This is the time to lift up your eyes unto the hills from whence cometh your help, i.e. you lift up your eyes when you focus your attention on your good. Remember, faith can do all things. *Thy faith hath made thee whole* (Matthew 9:22). *According to your faith be it unto you* (Matthew 9:29). You must appreciate the fact that your desire, idea, or dream is real, though it is invisible. To know that the idea is real, that it is a fact of consciousness, gives you faith and enables you to move over the waters of confusion, strife, and fear to a place of conviction deep in your own heart. Peter said, *Lord, if it be thou, bid me come unto thee on the water* (Matthew 14:28).

Ideas are our lords and masters. Ideas govern and rule us. The dominant idea which you now entertain is your lord; it generates its own emotion. Emotions compel you to express them. The dominant idea of success enthroned in the mind generates its own mood or feeling. This feeling compels you to right action, so that whatever you attempt under the mood of faith and confidence will be successful. The desire or idea of yours now is your lord. *Lord, if it be thou, bid me come unto thee upon the water* (Matthew 14:28). Mentally appropriate your desire, kiss it, love it, let it captivate your mind; feel the reality of it.

Is your desire lofty, inspiring, and wonderful enough to lead you forward? This ideal of yours is real, just as the idea of a radio was real in the mind of the inventor; or the idea of an automobile was real in the mind of Ford; or the idea of a house is real in the mind of an architect. It is not idle fancy or a daydream.

Peter is within you, i.e. *Peter* is faith, perseverance, stick-to-it-iveness, and an abiding trust in an Almighty Power which responds to man's thought and belief. This Formless Awareness within you takes the shape of your belief and conviction. It is really all things to all men. It is strength to you if you need strength; it is guidance if you need guidance; it is food and health, also.

Everyone has faith in something. What is your faith? Let it be faith in all things good, a joyous expectancy of the best, and a firm belief inscribed in your heart that Infinite Intelligence will lead you out of your difficulty and show you the way. You have a firm conviction now in the Power of God to solve your problems and heal you. This faith in God enables you to walk with confidence over all the waters of fear, doubt, worry, and imaginary dangers of all kinds. You now know that error and fear are false beliefs without power. You know these negative states are false and groundless. Paul says, *Faith is the substance of things hoped for, the evidence of things not seen* (Hebrews 11:1). It is from faith or feeling that all things flow.

When you look down you see mud, but when you look up you see the stars! Similarly, when you say, "There is no way out; I have no chance," you are looking, like Peter, at the winds of confusion, fear, and human opinion; but when he remembers where his power is, *he looks up at Jesus*, meaning that he looks at the solution, the way out, the happy ending and ignores the adverse winds of human intellect and the waves of mass mind.

The man of faith puts his trust in the Invisible Power within him. He knows this is the Kingdom of the Real. He knows that his ideal is real in the Inner Kingdom and that his faith or feeling will cause the formless or the invisible to take on form as a condition, event or experience. This is why the man of faith walks upon the waters and moves in confidence and understanding to the promised land—his cherished goal. Faith is accepting as true what your reason and intellect deny.

All great scientists, mystics, artists, poets, and inventors are gifted or possessed by an abiding faith and trust in the Invisible Powers within.

Faith is trust. You trusted your mother when you were in her arms; you looked into her eyes and you saw love there. Your *Peter* is your faith and trust in God, and it should be even greater than faith in your mother.

As you read this, turn your desire or request over to the subjective mind within you, acknowledging in your heart that it has the answer and the "know how" of accomplishment, and that its ways are past finding out. When you are relaxed and peaceful, you will know you have succeeded in impregnating your deeper mind. Signs follow; the wave of peace is the sign; this is inner conviction. You now walk above all the waters of confusion, chaos, and false beliefs, because in a little while what you felt to be true will be experienced in a very concrete sense.

Troward says that if a thing is true, there is a way in which it is true. Look at the magic and miracle-working power of faith in your own life. Behold the miracle which takes place as you drink a glass of milk; it is transformed into tissue, muscle, bone, hair, and blood cells in your body by the Master Chemist within. Look within for your saviour. Your true saviour is the realization of your heart's desire. Blend these together and you have a holy covenant, a wedded bliss, the mystic marriage. Any idea or desire impregnated with love is invincible; this is working faith. Blend Peter (faith) and Jesus (desire) together, and the miracle will happen.

How to Pray
with a Deck of
Cards

No one actually knows the real origin of the mysterious and fascinating modern playing cards. There is an old legend about the origin of cards which relates that many thousands of years ago the Chinese sages gathered together under the leadership of a great sage to discuss the fact that vast legions of brutal invaders were pillaging and plundering the land. The question to be resolved was, "How shall we preserve the ancient wisdom from the destruction of the invaders?"

There were many suggestions: Some thought that the ancient scrolls and symbols should be buried in the Himalayan Mountains. Others suggested that the wisdom be deposited in monasteries in Tibet. Still others pointed out that the sacred temples of India were the ideal places for the preservation of the wisdom of their God.

The chief sage was silent during the entire discussion; in fact he went to sleep in the midst of their talk, and snored loudly, much to their dismay! He awakened in a little while, and said, "Tao [God] gave me the answer, and it is this: We will order the great pictorial artists of China—men gifted with Divine imagination (which is the workshop of God)—and tell them what we wish to accomplish. We will initiate them into the mysteries of Truth. They will portray or depict in picture form the great truths which shall be preserved for all time and for countless generations yet unborn. When they are finished with the dramatization of the great Truths, Powers, Qualities, and Attributes of God through a series of picture cards, we will tell the world about a new game that has been originated. Men throughout the world for all time will use them as a game of chance, not knowing that through this simple device they are preserving the sacred teaching for all generations." This was the origin of our own deck of cards.

Many research scholars are of the opinion that cards originated in Egypt, from which the name Gypsies is derived, a nomadic tribe who travel all over the face of the earth telling fortunes and divining by cards, etc. Whether they originated in China, India, or Egypt really does not matter; the point is that they represent deep and profound psychological and spiritual truths. It is generally agreed that our cards, a composite design, are derived form the ancient Tarot cards, believed to be devised by Hebrew mystics to portray symbolically how the Laws of God work in the cosmos and in man. They consist of wands, cups, swords, and pentacles, and twenty-two of the seventy-eight Tarot cards are called "trump" cards. There is a Hebrew letter or word attached to each card, which letter has a definite, specific meaning.

You can understand the inner meaning of the Bible by a knowledge of the Hebrew alphabet and the science of symbolism. The ancients said that if all the Bibles of the world were destroyed, the Eternal Verities and the Laws of Life could be resurrected through the pictorial imagery and symbolism of the

Tarot cards, from which our own cards are derived. The cards have been misused down through the ages for purposes of divination, but undoubtedly the original purpose of the cards was to convey deep and profound mystical truths to man. Divination by various means has gone on through the ages. Moses expelled haruspices, purification augurs, and those who put faith in sounds and voices. When we give heed and attention to the prophecies of evil, we are actually rejecting the First Cause—God—the Spirit within.

We must give supreme authority and recognition to the God-Presence within and become the true prophet, i.e. prophesy only the good. Our mood, our inner feeling and conviction of God's Presence and His Eternal Goodness will be made manifest in our world. Our moods and beliefs are our prophets. What we feel on the inside as true, we experience on the outside. If we start with God and realize that He rules supreme in our minds, there can be only one result—good—for God and Good are synonymous. The beginning and the end are always the same. Begin with God as Supreme Power and Boundless Love, and you will always be certain of the future. The future is always the present grown up. It is your thought made visible. You can be absolutely certain of your future if you will now, today, plant whatsoever things are true, lovely, noble, and God-like in the Garden of God—your own mind.

You mold, fashion, shape, and direct your own destiny. The future is already in your mind and may be changed by prayer, meditation, and mystic visioning. You can be brainwashed and hypnotized by others into believing their dire predictions of misfortune and loss, but you must remember you abdicated your authority and permitted your thoughts to move negatively, creating the thing you feared. "What I feared most has come upon me" (Job).

The minute you set up a rival to God in your mind, you are looking for trouble and asking for trouble. Your faith in God and

His Love is your good fortune, and from now on you believe and live in the constant expectancy of the best. What is true of God is true of you. It is wonderful!

DESCRIPTION OF THE CONTEMPORARY DECK OF CARDS

There are fifty-two playing cards and two extra cards called the "Jokers," and they are enclosed in a cover and sealed. It is necessary to break the seal to use the cards. This is symbolic of man, for every man is a book which is sealed. Man houses God—he is the tabernacle of the Living God, for God's tabernacle is with man. Within man is the God-Presence. All the Intelligence, Wisdom, and Power of the Infinite One are located in the depths of man, waiting to be resurrected. Man must break the seal and learn of the imprisoned splendour within. When man learns of the powers of his conscious and subconscious mind and the law of action and reaction, he has broken the seal and is beginning to realize that thoughts are things— that what he feels, he attracts, and that what he believes, he experiences. If you think in a certain way repeatedly, you form an impression or concept in the subconscious area of your mind which becomes a subconscious force governing your outer actions.

Man unveiled is Spirit, Mind. When you think of yourself apart from your body, your name, your nationality, home, and environment, what are you? Divest yourself now of your body, and you will say, "I am Spirit, I am Mind." You are mentally disrobing yourself or breaking the seal, and you find the Kingdom of God is within.

The Joker is the odd card and is usually rejected but, of course, is given greater value when used in playing a game. The Joker is God, and He is usually rejected by man, because the

average man has a God outside himself—a sort of anthropo-
morphic being living in the skies, a punishing, avenging
Deity—or he has a vague, confused concept of God which is
based on ignorance, fear, and superstition. The average man rejects the Joker or the Indwelling God; he refutes the fact that his
own consciousness is God to his world, and that he creates and
fashions his own future by his thoughts and feelings.

When you use the Joker or the Hidden Power within, it magnifies everything in your life. Begin to use the Divine Power
within you, and magnify your health, peace, happiness, and joy:
this is the meaning of the Joker. We can't afford to neglect the
Spiritual Power within. If we do not pray, meditate, commune
with God, and imbibe His Truths, we get immersed in the negative atmosphere of the world, such as fear, war, rumors of war,
man's inhumanity to man, business problems, newspaper head-
lines, etc. If we continue to feed mentally on all sorts of
troubles, sicknesses, calamities, all these thoughts reach a point
of fulfillment within us, resulting in the precipitation of sickness, disease, and all sorts of disorder in our lives.

It does not pay to reject the Stone of Truth. "The Stone
which the builders rejected is made head of the corner." Put
God back on the throne of your mind, claim His Guidance and
Direction, and become replenished from the standpoint of Truth
and Beauty.

There are fifty-two cards, which, when added together, form
the numeral 7. There are fifty-two weeks in the year, which
represents the end of a solar cycle. The cycle also takes place in
our own mind. When you entertain an idea, nourish it mentally,
and become absorbed in the reality of it, the idea passes from
your conscious mind to your subconscious, and the cycle is
completed, because you have impressed your subconscious with
your concept, idea, plan, or purpose. Whatever is impressed in
the subconscious will be expressed, and your cycle is completed.
When impregnation of the subconscious mind takes place, it is

called the "sixth day"; that is, your mental and emotional act is completed. This is followed by a rest, called the "seventh day," or the day of rest in God. There is always an interval of time between the impregnation of the subconscious and the external manifestation of your prayer. This period of time is referred to as the Sabbath, or inner certitude, which follows the joy of the answered prayer. The Sabbath Day is more fully explained in my book *Peace within Yourself.**

The pack consists of four suits: Clubs, Hearts, Spades, and Diamonds, symbolizing the spirtual, mental, emotional, and physical nature of man. The four suits represent also the four letters in the name Jehovah, which are Yod-He-Vau-He. "Yod" means I Am, or God, the Spirit within. "He" is your desire or mental picture. "Vau" means nail, or feeling; and the final "He" is the external manifestation of what you saw and felt within as true in your own mind. In simple, everyday language, all it means is that whatever the idea, concept, or mental image you entertain in your mind, if you feel it and acknowledge it, you shall experience the result, whether it be negative or positive.

The four suits of cards are telling you how to pray, for that is the way you bring all experiences, conditions, and events into your life. It is the way all things are made manifest in your world, and there is nothing experienced by you that is not made that way.

EACH SUIT: THIRTEEN CARDS

Three of each suit are picture cards, namely King, Queen, and Jack, and ten are spot cards, from Ace (or one) to ten inclusive. The King, Queen, and Jack refer to the Trinity—the Father, Mother, and Child—which is represented symbolically in all the

*Published by DeVorss & Company.

great religions of the world. In simple, everyday language, the idea or thought you have is the father, feeling is the mother, and the union of the two brings forth issue or a mental child, which could be a healing of the mind, body, pocketbook, or business problem. The simple answer as well as the simple prayer is always the best.

Another explanation of the King card is that you were born to be a King over your own mind, body, and circumstances. The illumined, conscious mind is King, for it orders, directs, and issues instructions to the Queen, the subconscious or subjective, feeling nature. The Jack represents your purified desire, idea, or plan not yet made manifest. There must, therefore, be a synchronous union of the conscious and subconscious mind with your desire, and if both are in agreement, it shall come to pass and nothing shall be impossible unto you.

There are ten spot cards. I shall explain the numeral 10 briefly: 1 represents the male, and 0 represents the female. The union of the two results in the creative act, mentally and spiritually speaking as well as physically. The ten spot cards represent the harmonious interaction of your conscious and subconscious mind along all four phases of your life—spiritual, mental, emotional, and material. The virtues of ten are infinite in number. The numeral 10 means God in infinite differentiation, because you can add countless zeros to the numeral 1.

THE PICTURE CARDS

These cards are double, indicating our dual nature; we are living in a mental and spiritual world and also in an objective or three-dimensional world. When the outside world displeases us, we can go to the realm of mind, pray, and identify with our ideal by nourishing it, and through frequent occupancy of the mind we will bring it to pass; then the outside and the inside become one, and we are at peace. We change the outside by changing the inside. The outer is always a reflection of the inner. "As within, so without." There are two ends to the stick, there is an inside and an outside to everything. Life is a Oneness functioning as duality; there is night and day, ebb and flow, male and female, hot and cold, peace and pain, health and sickness, objective and subjective, invisible and visible, positive and negative, matter and spirit, good and evil. The opposites are dual expressions of the same eternal principle, which is forever whole and perfect in Itself.

THE HEADDRESS

The kings wear beards, which symbolize Wisdom and the Power of God. The crowns portray authority and the regnancy of Spirit ruling in the mind of man. The King of Diamonds with hand uplifted indicates his allegiance to God—the One Power—and behind him is an axe, suggesting that the law of the subconscious is always exact, mathematical, and just. "As we sow so also shall we reap." The axe also is indicative of the negative reaction of the law if we violate the law of harmony or Divine order in our life. Think evil, evil follows; think good, good follows—that is the law. The King of Hearts with the sword in his hand indicates the sword of Truth. "Think not that I am come to send peace on earth; I come not to send peace, but a sword" (Matthew 10:34).

Truth comes into your mind to divide it and separate the debris from the Truths of God. Truth separates you from the old, false beliefs of the race, provoking an inner quarrel, thereby resolving all differences and enthroning peace in the heart. The King of Hearts has pierced his heart (subconscious mind) with the Eternal Truths. The three swords held respectively by the King of Clubs, King of Spades, and King of Hearts possess sheaths which allude to holding the torch of Truth aloft in all phases of our life—mental, emotional, and physical.

Clubs represent your thoughts and ideas, Hearts your feeling or emotional nature, Spades your deep conviction where you dig or implant ideas in your subconscious, and Diamonds the world, the external objectification of your internal thoughts, feelings, and beliefs. In other words, you have the story of prayer given to you in many ways in a deck of cards. When you look at the four Queens in your cards, you will notice they hold a flower, the symbol of purity, love, beauty, order, symmetry, and proportion. The heart is the chalice of God's love and Beauty, which is to remind us that we should fill our hearts with God's Love, and the flowers of beauty, peace, joy, and happiness will appear on the earth—our world.

The Queen of Spades (the dominant feeling in your subconscious) holds a torch in her hand. This is the Light that lighteth every man that cometh into the world. It is to remind you that the Infinite Intelligence of God is within your subconscious depths, and that by that Light you can walk through darkness. When your sense evidence tells you something is impossible, you see by an inner Light, your eyes are on the solution which the God-Wisdom will bring to you as you hold your faith in God aloft. Let this torch be a candle which forever shines upon your head.

The Jack of Spades holds an hourglass, indicating that we are moving through time and space on this three-dimensional plane, and that whatever idea you have conveyed to the subconscious will come forth in its own way and its own time, because its ways are past finding out. The ways of the subconscious are not your ways, and you do not know the hour or the day—that is the secret of your subconscious self. The feather held by the Jack of Hearts and the axe behind his head tell you symbolically of the Law and the Word—the feather is your concept or idea, and the law executes it. Make sure your plan conforms to the good of all, and that it hurts no one. When in trouble, think of God and His answer. He knows only the answer—this is the "feather's weight" that saves you.

The robes and vestments worn by the figures are beautiful, elegant, and colorful—they indicate the seven colors of the solar spectrum. White is the purity, wholeness, and perfection of God. White is called the mother of all colors. The colors on the cards tell us of the immaculate and unblemished Presence within us. Red indicates purified desire and divinity. Scarlet stands for enthusiasm and God-Intoxication. Purple indicates royalty, or God's Wisdom reigning supreme in our mind. Green stands for God's abundance and fruitful ideas and thoughts. Blue indicates the subconscious area of our mind or the Law of God. Yellow indicates the Power, Strength, and Glory of the Infinite One.

NUMBER OF CARDS IN EACH SUIT

There are thirteen cards in each suit to remind us of our twelve powers, twelve faculties. You and your twelve powers are symbolized by the number 13. It behooves us all to develop and discipline these powers, so that a God-like man appears on the earth who will unstop the ears of the deaf, open the eyes of the blind, and do all the things a son of God should do.

You have forty spot cards. Noah was forty days in the ark, Jesus fasted for forty days—all these stories are symbolic of the fast from the poisoned feast of race thoughts and false concepts, as well as of our mental absorption in the good we seek to bring to pass. The length of time it takes you to detach yourself from your problem and reach a conviction in your mind is called forty days, or the completion of a cycle of consciousness. Fast from poverty thoughts and feast on God's Abundance—reject the appearance of things, the verdict or opinion of others, and give all your attention to the idea of God's Opulence. Gradually you qualify your consciousness, whether it takes an hour, a week, or a month. Sooner or later you will succeed in impregnating your subconscious with the idea of wealth. You have fasted for forty days, and you will experience God's wealth in your world.

The rods held by the Jack of Clubs and the Jack of Diamonds indicate a measuring rod or the cubit. *Man* means mind or measurer. You are to measure and appropriate in your mind the Infinite Goodness and Love of God, for your concept of God is your concept of yourself. The idea I have is one that I must cube, and cube is "mother" in Hebrew. Mother your idea, love it, and make it alive; then you have a spiritual standard to measure all things by.

I wish to touch on the hanging leaf on the Jack of Clubs. Clubs refer to the ideas, plans, and purposes in your mind, the scheme, diagram, or blueprint. You will notice on the Jack of Clubs how he bows over. This is humility, giving all honor and glory to God. Our attitude should be, "Father, I thank thee that thou hast heard me; and I knew that thou hearest me always" (John 11:41).

It is generally agreed that the number value, mathematical quantities, colors, and symbolism of the playing cards have a very close connection with the Great Pyramid. The ancient mystics who devised playing cards thousands of years ago knew all about the rotation of the earth on its axis and were able to measure the heavens and the earth, all of which is portrayed in the cards and the Great Pyramid. Men like Job intuitively perceived the laws written in our hearts and inscribed in our inward parts. "Where wast thou when I laid the foundations of the earth? Declare, if thou hast understanding. Who hath laid the measures thereof, if thou knowest? Or who hath stretched the line upon it? Whereupon are the foundations thereof fastened? or who laid the corner stone thereof?" (Job 38:4–6).

Supreme Mastery of Fear

The Lord is my Light and my Salvation; whom shall I fear? the Lord is the strength of my life; of whom shall I be afraid?

—Psalm 27:1

For in the time of trouble he shall hide me in his pavilion: in the secret of this tabernacle shall he hide me: he shall set me up upon a rock.

—Psalm 27:5

Who is your Lord and master this very moment? Your Lord is your predominant mental attitude; it is your conviction or belief about yourself, people, and things. This Lord can be a tyrant. For example, if your mood is now one of resentment, that is your Lord or tyrant that governs all of your actions and all phases of your life. If you want to invest some money, buy a new house, or some property, while in this attitude you will do the wrong thing and say the wrong thing, because your

141

predominant mood is negative. The law is: "As within, so without." You are fearing your good, and you would react negatively. Fear is a lack of faith or trust in God, which is a denial of His omnipotence.

"The Lord is my light and my salvation." The Lord referred to is the Lord God, or the law of God or good. To put the law of good into operation—thereby banishing fear once and for all—enthrone in your mind the thoughts of power, courage, and confidence. These thoughts will generate a corresponding mood or feeling, which will banish the archenemy of your success and health.

Fear—this self-made enemy of yours—must be completely destroyed before the Lord God can shine through you. Your fear is the cloud that hides the sunshine of God. Men have made personal devils out of fear of the past, the present, and the future.

It is our attitude toward life that determines the experiences we are to meet. If we expect misfortune, we shall have it. Knowing the law of God or good, the truth student expects only good fortune. The world is not harsh; it may seem to be, because we fail to affirm or claim the Presence of God. Men fear criticism so much, that many of their most beautiful thoughts never see the light of day. To the man who believes that God is the only Presence and the only Power, there is no past; he knows that if he believes in the power of the past, he is disbelieving in God. God is the Eternal Now; there is no future and no past in God.

This is the Gospel—the good tidings. There is no such thing as past karma; there is only man's foolish, false belief in it. *"Now is the day of salvation!"* The Kingdom of Heaven is at hand. Your good, your health, and your success are here now; feel the reality of them; thrill to them. Enter into the conviction that you are now the being you long to be.

The only guilt there is, is the consciousness of guilt. "Though your sins are as scarlet, they shall be white as snow;

though red like crimson, they shall be as wool." This is the good news. The only moment that matters is the present. You can live only in the now, experience in the now, plan in the now, and think in the now. Whatever you are planning or dreading, you are planning it now. When you realize that every form of lack and limitation is the result of your wrong thinking and feeling, you shall know the Truth that sets you free. The mountains will be removed.

Aboriginal tribes and primitive man feared nature. Modern man fears his fellow man. To a great extent we have dispelled the ghosts of ancient days. We have combatted the plagues, and we will soon control the elements. Man is doped by modern propaganda. Some men are afraid to live and afraid to speak. Mothers fear for their children. All this is due to superstitious belief that there is another power to challenge God.

The only evil there is, is due to a lack of knowledge of the laws of life. If we put our hand on an open wire, we get a shock, but if it is insulated properly, we do not; the evil or shock was due to our ignorance. Any man will admit that electricity is not evil; it blesses humanity in countless ways. Electricity is used to play music, drive trains, fry eggs, vacuum the floors, and light the world. Evil or fear is our misapplication and incomplete comprehension of the Omnipresence of God or good. Where fear is, love cannot be, for error cannot dwell with understanding.

The wealthy fear they are going to lose; the poor fear they shall not gain. The only wealth and the only security are found in the consciousness in which we abide. If we are conscious of being wealthy, nothing in all the world can stop us from being prosperous in our bodies and affairs. The things men fear are unreal. Only the One alone is real; only the One alone is Law; only the One alone is Truth.

The jungle doctor of old has passed on many of his superstitions; consequently, countless cults today instill fear into the minds of many individuals. Let us face the facts. The cause of most fear is man's fear of his fellow man. Many men pray together on Sunday, and prey on each other on Monday.

The answer to the problem is understanding. All fear is due to ignorance. In order to express harmony, we must think and feel harmonious thoughts. When we enter into the mood of success, confidence, and happiness, we will express similar results in all phases of our life. When man knows that every form of discord, sickness, and lack is due to wrong thinking, he will know the Truth which sets him free.

Learn to imagine the thing desired, and then feel the reality of the state sought. This is the easiest and quickest way to get results. Some get results by convincing themselves of the Truth—that God is the only Presence and the only Power; this is one of the most wonderful things in all the world to know.

Regardless of the cause of the fear, you have no one to treat or heal but yourself. You have to convince yourself that you are now expressing Life, Love, and Truth. Let us not fear anything or anybody; let us be busy radiating courage, confidence, and power. In this way we will crush all obstacles in our path, and the mountains will be cast into the sea.

We are one with Infinite Power. If we say we are weak or infirm, we are telling a falsehood about God. Fear turns the love of God or good away from us in the same way that a poverty consciousness attracts poverty in health, money, business, and love relationships. Man must stop preaching fear to his fellow man and unite in teaching all of the Truth.

The Truth is that there is no hell, devil, purgatory, limbo, or damnation of any kind. Moreover, there is no past karma which we must expiate here; there is no future evil. God is the Eternal Now! This is one of the most dramatic and significant statements in the whole Bible: "Now is the day of Salvation." This very moment all that you need do is turn to God and claim for yourself that which you long to be; accept it, believe it, and go thy way rejoicing. "Though your sins be as scarlet, they shall be white as snow; though red like crimson, they shall be as wool." "Forgive till seventy times seven." "This day thou shalt be with me in paradise."

Let us stop instilling fear into the minds of youth; let us teach them the real facts. We must not preach religious tolerance except we live it. We must teach the Truth. We must not distort the Truth so that we may hold a position, or because we are afraid that the people will not come back; this type of fear results in spiritual stagnation and frustration. We must keep our eye on the Kingdom of Heaven, not upon the kingdom of earth. We must teach man to know the Truth, and the Truth shall make him free. The Truth is: Man is belief expressed!

There is no fear where faith in God rules. There is no fear of man where integrity rules in one's consciousness. There is no fear of criticism where the consciousness of kindliness enters into the mind of man. Religion is goodwill in action or the application of the Golden Rule. We have seen, therefore, that fear is man's basic weakness, and it is based solely on ignorance.

"In time of trouble he shall hide me in his pavilion; in the secret of his tabernacle shall he hide me: he shall set me up upon a rock." The pavilion is a canopy or covering. This means the covering shall be the garment of God (mood of good). Think about God. Begin to ask yourself, "What does God mean to me?" Realize that God, or I Am, is the Life in you, your own consciousness, and It is omnipotent.

For example, if a man is in prison, he automatically desires freedom. God and good are synonymous. He begins to think of this Infinite Power and Wisdom within him; he knows that It has ways of freeing him which he knows not of. He imagines, therefore, the opposite, which is freedom. Though he is behind bars, in meditation he imagines that he is at home talking to his loved ones. He hears familiar voices and feels the welcoming kisses of his children on his cheek. This is *hiding in the pavilion*. The prisoner actualizes this state by feeling the joy of being home. It is possible to rise high enough in consciousness in five or ten minutes to bring about a subjective conviction. This is the meaning of *"In the secret of his tabernacle shall he hide me."* The law is: Whatever is impressed is expressed; consequently, the prison doors are open for him in ways that he knows not of. "My ways are past finding out."

We read in the Scriptures: "Fear not, little flock, it is your Father's good pleasure to give you the kingdom." Jesus tells us this kingdom is within us—this Kingdom of Heaven or harmony is within every one of us. Infinite Wisdom, Divine Intelligence, and Infinite Power are available to all men, because God is within them, and He is the very Life of them. Anyone can prove to himself that the Kingdom of Heaven is at hand. It is right here now. Jesus saw it, and lived in it. We are color blind; that is why we do not see it. The blindness is due to ignorance and fear. We are blinded by centuries of false beliefs, superstition, creeds, and dogmas. The Truth is so shrouded by false dogmas that we have created God and a heaven of our making. God is to us what we believe Him to be. Man has created a horrendous creature in the skies; he visualizes a God of caprice and vengeance, or an inscrutable being who sends wars, plagues, etc. We create our own hell and our own heaven, based upon our concept of God. Anyone can prove that the Kingdom of Heaven is at hand.

Let me tell you the story of a young girl who proved it. She was living with a father who came home drunk every night and sometimes treated her brutally. She lived in constant fear of her father. She kept house for him. Due to frustration, her face was covered with acne.

We are not living with people; we are living with our concept of them. Realizing this truth, the girl in meditation closed her eyes and dwelt on the God Power within her. She no longer clothed her father in the garment or mood of a drunkard. Instead, she saw a loving, kind father who had perfect balance, poise, and equilibrium. She clothed him in righteousness, and her judgment was "a robe and a diadem," which means that she saw her father as he ought to be. The fact that her father was drinking heavily meant that he was seeking escape to conceal an inferiority complex or a subjective sense of loss. In other words, he was trying to run away from himself.

This girl spoke the word which healed him. She relaxed her whole body, closed her eyes, and began to say to herself, "How would I feel if my father were loving, kind, and peaceful?" She dwelt on the solution, which generated a mood of peace, confidence, and joy within her; this was clothing him in righteousness. Her judgment was "as a robe and a diadem."

When you pass judgment, you come to a decision. It is the final verdict, and you are the judge passing judgment; "As I hear, I judge." Her verdict was an inner hearing or feeling wherein she saw her father smiling, happy, and joyous; she imagined he was telling her how wonderful he felt, and that he had found peace, balance, and poise. She also heard him telling her how wonderful she was; she thrilled to the fact that her father was healed and made whole. "He wore a seamless robe"—no holes, no patches, and no seams. This means she meditated on the mood of love, peace, and oneness with her ideal. All doubts and fears were absent (judgment as "a robe"). "Judgment as a diadem" means she gave "beauty for ashes," which signifies she saw beauty in her father and felt it. Beauty was expressed on the screen of space.

After one week's treatment her father was completely healed; moreover, he was a changed man. His attitude was completely transformed, and the two are devoted to each other. She proved the Kingdom of Heaven (harmony and peace) is at hand NOW. What are we afraid of? "If God be for us, who can be against us?" The thing you fear does not exist.

For example, a man lives in fear that his business will fail. His business is not failing; neither is he in bankruptcy. Business is as usual, and it may be booming; the failure does not exist save in his imagination. Job said, "What I fear most has come upon me." Job is every man who walks the earth. Therefore as the successful businessman continues to sustain the mood of failure, sooner or later his mood crystallizes into a subjective conviction or impression.

Any feeling impressed on the subconscious mind is made manifest by an immutable law of life. The subconscious, being impersonal and no respecter of persons, says, "John wants to fail in business." So it proceeds in ways that he, John, knows not of to bring this failure to pass. Everyone realizes that he brought this failure on himself through imagination and feeling.

I knew a lady who read of an airplane crash. She was contemplating a trip by air to Los Angeles, but she lived in fear of an accident. A negative thought cannot do you any harm except it is energized by a charge of fear. It must be emotionalized before it becomes subjective. This lady did not know what she was doing; she was ignorant of the laws of life. This ignorance is the cause of all of our accidents and misfortunes. Having imagined herself in an airplane accident, and having emotionalized this negative thought with fear, it became a subjective state. When she took the trip two months later, she had the accident that she *knew* she would have.

If a woman fears her husband is going to leave her, there is a way to conquer her mood. The fear is a negative feeling which is communicated to him. If he does not know the laws of life, her conviction of him will be made manifest. In other words, he will do the thing she feared he would do, because this was her conviction of him. Instead of this fear, she supplants it by seeing her husband radiating peace, health, and happiness. In meditation morning and night, she radiates the mood of love and peace and feels that her husband is the most wonderful man in all the world. She feels that he is loving, kind, and devoted. She imagines he is telling her how wonderful she is, and how happy, free, and balanced he is. Her mood of fear is now changed to a mood of love and peace. This is the Spirit of God moving in her behalf. As she continues to do this, this mood jells within her. She now knows, "He never faileth," and that "Perfect love casteth out fear."

Our daily prayer or daily mood must be one of joyous expectancy or a confident expectancy of all good things; this is our greatest prayer. If we expect the best, the best will come to us. It is our mood that is vital.

The modern metaphysician of today teaches that God is the life principle within man. If you feel full of confidence and trust, this is the movement of the Spirit of God within you, and It is all-powerful. "None shall stay its hand and say unto it, What doest thou?" Man's own consciousness is God; there is no other God. By consciousness is meant existence, life, and awareness.

You, the reader, know that you exist. This knowing that you exist is God. What you are aware of is your concept of God. Each must ask himself, "What am I aware of?" The answer to this question is his belief about God. It is what he knows about God. When he says, "I am aware of want, I am fearful, I am sick," these are lies and have no truth in them. When man says, "I am fearful," he is saying God is full of fear, which is nonsensical. When he says, "I am in want," he is relating a lie and a denial of God's abundance and infinite supply. His faith is in failure, and he succeeds in being a failure. He believes in a lie, but he cannot prove the lie. The false condition seems real as long as he dwells upon it. When he ceases to believe it, he is free and healed.

Write a New Name in the Book of Life

THE BOOK OF LIFE is your subconscious mind, and you are always writing in that Book of Life based on your habitual thinking and imagining. Shakespeare said, "What is in a name?" Well, when I mention your name, it indicates your particular sex, your nationality, your background, your training, your education, your financial structure, your social status, and all things appertaining to you.

Shakespeare wrote many plays. *Romeo and Juliet*, for example, is a drama of your own conscious and subconscious mind. And when your conscious and subconscious mind work harmoniously, peacefully, and joyfully together, the children of that union are happiness, peace, health, abundance, and security. The disharmonious relationship of the conscious and subconscious mind brings misery, suffering, pain, sickness, and disease into your life.

Abram left Ur of Chaldea. Ur means sorcery, black magic, worship of stars, idols, and all that sort of thing. Abram changed his name to Abraham, meaning the father of the multitude, indicating the one God, the one Presence and Power.

We are all children of the one God. That's the unity of all life. All men and women are brothers—same mind, same spirit, and same substance. Therefore to hurt another is to hurt yourself; and to bless another is to bless yourself.

You can write a new name, a new estimate, a new blueprint of yourself. Get a new concept of yourself. Is it great enough, noble enough, or grand enough to redeem you, to bring about an inner transformation of your heart, your mind, and your whole being? Today people have many idols, just as they had in Chaldea years ago. Superstition is rampant. They still have false gods, such as "The weather is going to give me a cold," or "If I wet my feet, I am going to get pneumonia." Some are afraid of germs, so that when someone sneezes, they feel they may get the virus. If you ask the exposed person, "Did you get the virus this year?" the response is, "No, not yet." The infection is anticipated, though. What you expect, you always get.

Some say, "I don't know the right Congressman. I have no pull. I can't get that job." They are denying the Creative Power within them. They say It is omnipotent and supreme, yet all the time they are denying It. If It is supreme and omnipotent, there is nothing to oppose It or challenge It. Therefore you should say, "Infinite Spirit opens up the door for me, revealing to me my hidden talents and showing me the way I should go." That's exactly what the Infinite Spirit will do for you.

There are Congressmen who speak and touch wood when they talk about something negative, as if the wood had some power. Do you give power to other people? To the atmosphere? To the weather? All these things are impotent. They have no power. The power is in you.

Saul's name was changed to Paul. The meaning of Paul is the "Little Christ," and many miracles were wrought by the hand of Paul. Paul was illumined on the road to Damascus, which means a sack of blood, or rebirth. This means a mystical illumination where your mind, or intellect, is flooded with the light of God and you are a transformed man. Sometimes this takes place in the twinkling of an eye, like that which was experienced by St. Theresa and many others.

Paul became a changed man. He was no longer the murderer who sent people to death. He was transformed. He was illumined from On High. You can go to court and change your name every year if you wish. It doesn't mean anything. It is absolutely meaningless. You must change your nature, your disposition, your viewpoint, your concept of yourself. There must be an inner transformation. Then, of course, you have changed your name, or your nature.

Some time ago a man came to see me who was cynical and a sourpuss who would snarl at his secretary and at the salesman when he came in. If someone said, "It's a good day," he would say, "What's good about it?" When he came down to breakfast in the morning, he would hold the paper up in front of himself lest he see his wife. He would always criticize the bacon and the eggs. He was just a plain sourpuss—nasty and ugly.

He went to a psychologist, and the psychologist said, "I'll tell you what you do. You can change your whole nature. When you come down in the morning, kiss your wife and tell her she looks lovely and that the food is delicious, and she'll probably faint." The man said, "Well, I'll be a hypocrite if I do that." The psychologist said, "Go ahead. Start it anyhow. Break the ice in your heart. When you go into the office, tell the secretary how beautiful her hair is, or her eyes—there must be something lovely about her. And be genial, courteous, and affable to the salesman."

After a month's time, as he practiced these things, gradually they sank into his subconscious mind and he became transformed—genial, affable, amiable, and philosophical. People said, "What happened to that fellow?" Others said, "He's in love." Well, I guess he was—in love with the Higher Self.

"He that guided me this far will open up the rest of the way." That's a magnificent truth. A teacher wrote me from Alabama, and I gave him that simple truth. He said his building was three-quarters finished and now there was a strike; he didn't have the money, and what was he going to do? "He that guided me this far will open up the rest of the way."

He said, " 'That' is not correct. You should say, 'He *who* guided me will open up the rest of the way.' " I said, "No. I meant 'that' literally." It was not a slip. It was deliberate, because I am dealing with a Principle, an impersonal Presence which is no respecter of persons, a universal Presence and Power available to all men. The cutthroat, beggar, thief, holy man, atheist or agnostic—any man can tap it. Any man can use it.

God is not a person, so we don't say, "Our Father *who* art in Heaven." We say, "Our Father *which* art in Heaven, indicating an impersonal Presence and Power—an Infinite Life and Infinite Intelligence. So, you see, he had a concept of a God-man up in the sky somewhere. He practiced, however, what I taught him to do, and he found that he attracted the necessary funds to complete the building.

This Universal Presence creates out of Itself by means of Its becoming that particular thing. In other words, God becomes man by believing Himself to be man. God creates a being out of Himself capable of returning glory, light and love to Himself. Abraham knew the Creative Power. He was aware of it, and he demonstrated It in his life. He believed that the Spirit would guide and direct him, which, of course, It did.

Plato, Aristotle, Plotinus, etc., all spoke of God as Infinite

Mind and Infinite Intelligence, but they didn't tell you how to use the Presence and Power for guidance, for harmony, for prosperity, for success, or how to heal yourself with It. It was a satisfactory intellectual conclusion—very interesting. But they didn't tell you how to use It in everyday practice.

If you believe you are an old worm of the dust, people will step on you and will treat you the way you treat yourself. If you are cruel and nasty to yourself, the world will be cruel and nasty to you. As within, so without. Realize you are a son or a daughter of the Living God. You are heir to all of God's riches. Realize you should exalt God in the midst of you mighty to heal. How could you feel inferior if you knew that you are a daughter of the Infinite, that you are a darling of God, and that God loves you and cares for you? God is the Life Principle, or the Living Spirit within you, which created you and watches over you when you are sound asleep, because He who watches over you neither slumbers nor sleeps.

There are a great many people who work very hard, but they nevertheless fail in life. The reason is that they have a subconscious pattern of failure, or they believe they should fail. Sometimes they think a jinx is following them. They feel inferior. Perhaps they were told when they were young, "You'll never amount to anything. You'll always be a failure. You are stupid. You are dumb." These thoughts were accepted by their impressionable mind and now these thoughts have a life of their own in the subconscious mind, and are experienced by them.

But man can change his life. These subconscious or irrational impulses act long after the events which caused them have been forgotten. Man can feed the subconscious mind with something new. He can say, "I'm born to succeed; the Infinite cannot fail." He can feed his subconscious such life-giving patterns as: "Divine law and order govern my life; Divine peace fills my soul; Divine love saturates my mind; Divine right action reigns supreme; Infinite Intelligence guides and directs me in all my ways—It is a lamp unto my feet and a light upon my path."

When you are angry, suspicious, or full of fear, these emotions are negative and destructive. They snarl up in the subconscious mind, and they cause you to do the wrong thing and to say the wrong thing. When you want to be happy, you're sad; when you want to do the right thing, you do the wrong thing. This is true when you are under the sway of negative and destructive emotions, for whatever you do then will be wrong.

So you can write a new name in the Book of Life. The Book of Life, as we explained to you, is the law of your own subconscious. The Bible says, *I saw in the right hand of Him that sat on the throne a book written within and on the backside, sealed with seven seals. And I saw a strong angel proclaiming with a loud voice, Who is worthy to open the book, and to loose the seals thereof? And no man in heaven, nor in earth, neither under the earth, was able to open the book, neither to look thereon. And I wept much, because no man was found worthy to open and to read the book, neither to look thereon* (Revelation 5:1–4).

Now the book written within and on the backside is your objective and subjective mind. You have a conscious and subconscious mind. Whatever thoughts, beliefs, opinions, theories, or dogmas you write, engrave, or impress on your subconscious mind you experience as objective manifestations—as circumstances, conditions, and events. What we write on the inside we experience on the outside. We have two sides of our lives—objective and subjective, visible and invisible, thought and its manifestation.

The seven seals are the seven states of consciousness. Our concept passes through seven degrees of awareness whereby we spiritualize our five senses by turning inward to the Spiritual Power. Then we get our conscious and subconscious mind to agree and synchronize. When there is no longer any doubt in your conscious or subconscious mind, your prayer is always answered. You break the seven seals when you discipline your five senses and get the two phases of your mind to agree.

There are seven seals. The first is sight. This means to see the truth about any situation. See perfect health where sickness is; see harmony where discord is; love where hatred is. Then you are seeing the truth, and you are disciplining your faculty of sight.

The second is hearing. You hear the glad tidings, the truths of God. You hear your mother tell you what you long to hear— that the miracle of God has happened; that she is healed. In other words, you don't see her in a hospital as being ill. You hear the opposite. You hear her tell you about her perfect health. Then you are hearing the truth.

The third is smell. You smell the truth by coming to a definite decision, realizing that God who made your body can also heal it. You reject all other "food" as unfit for mental consumption. A dog smells food; if it is unsavory, he rejects it. Likewise, reject all thoughts, ideas, and opinions that do not fill your soul with joy.

The fourth is taste. You taste the sweet savor of God. You taste the truth by appropriating the ideas or truths of God in your mind through meditation and through frequent occupancy of the mind regarding the perfect outcome you want.

The fifth is the joy when you touch mentally and emotionally the answered prayer, while feeling the reality of it.

The remaining two seals are your conscious and subconscious mind. When you succeed in disciplining the five senses, the male and female principles in your own mind begin to interact harmoniously. A Divine marriage takes place between your desire and your emotion, and a child comes forth from the union, which is the joy of the answered prayer.

That's the Book of Life that people are talking about. If someone should photograph your subconscious mind, they could see your future, your past, and your present thinking. The future is your present thoughts grown up. You can always change the future by changing the present. Feast on whatsoever things are true, lovely, noble, and God-like. Think these thoughts with conviction. The old thoughts will die. They'll fade away. They'll be obliterated, expunged from your deep mind, because the lower is subject to the higher.

Think of everything lovely and of good report. Get new thoughts, new ideas, regarding principles and the eternal verities. Remember, your subconscious mind does not accept your idle wishes, dreams or hopes. It accepts your convictions—what you really believe deep down in your heart.

What do you believe? Do you believe in the goodness of God in the land of the living, and the guidance of God, and the harmony of God, and the love of God, and the abundance of God? If you do, all these things will come to pass because to believe is to live in the state of what is believed in. It's to accept something as true.

Look at your spiritual heritage. We are all children of the I AM, as Moses says. Within you is the real nature or the real name, because you are pronouncing it all day long. I AM. It's called Om in India. The Bible says, *I AM THAT I AM* (Exodus 3:14). Moses said, *I AM hath sent me unto you* (Exodus 3:14).

Realize I AM sends you to your business tomorrow, to a tough assignment, to solve it, to overcome it. The engineer, when he meets with a pressing problem, realizes I AM has sent him there to solve the problem. The engineer grapples with the problem courageously, and he sees the solution.

We are all children of the I AM (God). Whatever you attach to I AM, you become. If you say, I am no good, I'm a flop, I'm a failure, I'm going deaf, I'm going blind, I'm nobody, whatever you attach to it you become. Reverse it and say, ''I am happy, joyous, and free. I am illumined; I am inspired; I am strong; I am powerful. 'Let the weak say, I am strong.' 'Let the widow say,

it is well.' I am a son [or daughter] of the Living God. I am heir
to all of God's riches. I am born to win, to succeed, for the Infinite cannot fail. I am a tremendous success. I am absolutely
outstanding. I am unique, and there is no one in all the world
like me."

Why don't you claim the above and write these truths in
your heart and inscribe them in your inward parts? *He that hath
an ear, let him hear what the Spirit saith unto the churches: To
him that overcometh will I give to eat of the hidden manna, and
will give him a white stone, and in the stone a new name written, which no man knoweth saving he that receiveth it* (Revelation 2:17).

Manna is a symbol of the bread of Heaven. *I am the living
bread which came down from Heaven* (John 6:51). It's the bread
of peace, of harmony; it's the blessed bread of God. Eat the bread
of inspiration and guidance, for no man can live in this world today without spiritual food. You may sit down to dinner and have
the choicest food but still be hungry for peace, harmony, love,
inspiration, and guidance.

Manna is a symbol of inspiration, of strength, of power, and
of wisdom. It will feed you in the desert of loneliness, of unhappiness, because the greatest desert of the world is not the Sahara;
it's under the hat of man. There is very little growing there but
weeds of ignorance, fear, and superstition. Buddha asked God
the cause of all misery, suffering, crime, and sickness in the
world. The answer he received was "ignorance," for ignorance
is the only sin, and all punishment is the consequence.

Call on this Presence and Power. It will answer you. It will
be with you in trouble. It will set you On High, because you
have known Its name or nature. The nature of Infinite Intelligence is to respond to you. Turn within to the Fountain of Life
and feel refreshed from the standpoint of truth. You can be
replenished there. *Come ye to the waters, and he that hath no
money; come ye, buy, and eat; yea, come, buy wine and milk*

without money and without price (Isaiah 55:1). The price is recognition, acceptance, conviction. The price is to honor God and to believe in Him. That's the only price you pay.

If you don't honor God and recognize Him, it's just the same as if the Presence were not there. You can eat of the bread of peace, of joy, of faith, and of confidence in the only Power there is. Your confidence and faith should not be in creeds, dogma, and traditions. Believe that whatever you impress on your subconscious will be expressed as form, function, experience, and event. Then you are learning to know yourself a little better.

A new name is a new disposition, a new perspective, a new insight. You can affirm, "God loves me and cares for me. I am illumined from On High." You can claim right action. You can claim, "The wisdom of God anoints my intellect and I am now writing this with my conscious pen into my subconscious mind. Whatever I inscribe in my subconscious mind becomes effective and functional."

You are here to solve problems. The reason you have problems and challenges is that you are here to discover your Divinity and sharpen your mental and spiritual tools; otherwise you'd never discover yourself.

There are failures in life, yes! That's why you had an eraser at the end of your pencil when you went to school. Everybody knew you were going to make mistakes. Through the mistakes, however, you learned how to add and subtract as well as many, many other things.

You must have a basis for thinking constructively. When you know that thoughts are things and that what you feel you attract, and that what you imagine you become, then you begin to think constructively because you realize, "My thought is creative—not because it's my thought, but because it is thought."

"Nothing can give you peace but the triumph of principles," wrote Emerson. Quimby said that a child is like a little blank tablet; and the uncles, and the aunts, and the clergyman, and everybody else comes along and scribbles something on it. This is easy to do because the little mind, of course, is impression-able, malleable, and open to all the beliefs, opinions, creeds, dogmas, superstition, ignorance, and fear of the parents. The child grows up in the image and the likeness of the dominant mental, emotional, and spiritual climate of the home.

Who is scribbling on your mind today? Does your mother-in-law, father-in-law, or some in-law scribble something on your mind? Do they disturb you? Does someone tell you you are go-ing to fail? Or do you reject it and say, ''You don't know what you are saying. I can't fail. How could I fail? The Infinite is within me. I am born to win. I am a success in my prayer life, in my relationship with people, and in my chosen work.'' The minute you affirm the above, the Power will respond to you.

How could the Infinite fail? Where is the Infinite? Within you. And you are born to win, to overcome, to triumph. You are here to go from glory to glory, and from octave to octave, for there is no end to the glory which is man.

Is the columnist writing something in your mind? Or are you writing the truths of God, which are the same yesterday, to-day, and forever? What are you writing in your mind every day? Some people write grief, despair, hopelessness, loneliness, etc. Inscribe the conviction that you are worthy, that you are ade-quate, that you are full of faith and confidence in the only Power there is, and that you know you are inspired from On High, and you believe implicitly that God is guiding you in all your ways and is a Lamp unto your feet and a Light upon your path.

Your subconscious mind, which is the Book of Life, will receive these impressions, viewpoints, opinions, and convic-tions because you are sincere, because you mean them. Whatever you think, feel, and believe to be true, your subcon-scious mind will bring to pass—good or bad.

Inscribe in your mind harmony, health, wholeness, beauty, peace, perfection, and right action. These are principles. You do not create these truths, but you activate them and make them effective and functional when you affirm them. Stir up the gifts of God within you.

Anything that fills you with faith, with confidence, with joy, and with enthusiasm has power over you, and it governs your conduct. Enthusiasm governs all your activities, because enthusiasm means "possessed by God." You will never go so far as when you are possessed by the One—the Beautiful and the Good.

You are a mental and a spiritual being, because when you say I AM, you are announcing the Presence of the Living God. You have always lived. A billion years from now you will be alive, because Life was never born and will never die; water wets it not, fire burns it not, wind blows it not away. You are alive, and that life is God's life. God is Life; therefore, you have always lived.

Are you the same person you were five years ago? Ten years ago? Twenty-five years ago? No, you're not. Are you the same person you were when you were three months old or a year old? You have had hundreds of reincarnations since you were born. Reincarnation is Spirit making Itself manifest at higher levels. So, at five years of age you were different; at 10, at 20, and at 30. If I showed you photographs of every month of your life, you would hardly recognize yourself in some of them.

You are not the same as you were six months ago. You have a new concept of God, of Life, of the universe—a new estimate, a new blueprint, a new insight. You don't talk the same; you don't walk the same or think the same. Your life is going from glory to glory. When you go on to the next dimension, you still go on from octave to octave. You can't be less tomorrow than you are today, for life goes not backward nor tarries with yesterday.

Write, "I go from glory to glory. I go from octave to octave." Write these truths in your life, because you are alive and you are always implanting something new in your deeper mind.

I receive many letters, a few of which say, ''You will be cast into a lake of fire because you are telling people on your radio program that each man is his own saviour, that God indwells him, and that all he has to do is contact this God-Presence and It will lead him, guide him, and solve his problems for him. You also say that every man answers his own prayers. Some day you will burn in the lake of fire for all eternity for saying these things.'' Then they quote the Bible and say, *"For God so loved the world, that He gave his only begotten Son, that whosoever believeth in him should not perish, but have everlasting life"* (John 3:16).

All this is based on a lack of understanding. Everybody is the only begotten Son. We are all begotten of the Only One. There is only One. Your only begotten Son, spiritually speaking, is your desire. If you are sick, health is your saviour. You have a desire for health. Realization of your desire is your saviour. If you are lost in the woods, guidance is your saviour. If you are imprisoned, freedom is your saviour. If you are dying of thirst, water is your saviour. So every man who is able to contact the God-Presence is, of course, his own saviour.

The lake of fire mentioned in the Bible is no literal fire, of course. The Bible is a spiritual book. It is speaking in spiritual, mental, allegorical, figurative, idiomatic, and mystical language. When you go to a hospital in the psychotic ward, or in any mental institution, you will find people there burning in the lake of fire. The lake, of course, is your subconscious mind. The fire means they are seething with jealousy, hate, resentment, hostility, and anger. They are burning up their tissues and their hearts with these negative emotions.

A psychotic is tormented, isn't he? He's on fire with his own misery. Some people are on fire with their own hatred, resentment, hostility, etc. Of course, they are living in a lake of fire created by themselves, because every man creates his own hell and his own heaven. Omar said:

I sent my Soul through the Invisible,
Some letter of that After-Life to spell:
And by and by my Soul return'd to me,
And answer'd "I Myself am Heav'n and Hell."

Anger, depression, fear, and foreboding are the inner fires. The doctor tells you these emotions give you ulcers, high blood pressure, cancer, and arthritis. Hate will give you arthritis if you keep it up; it will bring about changes, bring on calcareous deposits in your tissues, and play havoc with you. Sometimes jealousy will drive a person absolutely insane, because there is no more destructive poison than jealousy. It is called the green-eyed monster and is the greatest of all mental poisons.

Therefore sow for yourself treasures in heaven, where the moth and the rust do not consume, and where thieves cannot break through and steal. Sow for yourself harmony, health, peace, and beauty. Write in your heart the truths of God. What will you write? Write . . . *whatsoever things are true, whatsoever things are honest, whatsoever things are just, whatsoever things are pure, whatsoever things are lovely, and whatsoever things are of good report. If there be any virtue, if there be any praise, think on these things now and forever more* (Philippians 4:8).

The Song of Triumph

Tell me, O thou whom my soul loveth, where thou feedest, where thou makest thy flock to rest at noon?

Behold, thou art fair, my love; behold, thou art fair; thou hast doves' eyes.

He brought me to the banqueting house, and his banner over me was love.

His left hand is under my head, and his right hand doth embrace me.

My beloved spake, and said unto me, Rise up, my love, my fair one, and come away.

For lo, the winter is past, the rain is over and gone;

The flowers appear on the earth; the time of the singing of birds is come, and the voice of the turtledove is heard in our land;

Arise, my love, my fair one, and come away.

My beloved is mine, and I am his; he feedeth among the lilies.

Until the day break, and the shadows flee away.

—The Song of Solomon

IT IS INCONCEIVABLE that any anthology could be written wherein The Song of Solomon was not included. It is really one of the most inspired parts of the Bible. The Song of Solomon reveals God as Universal love. It is ecstatic and thrilling.

In order to lead the triumphant life, you must be moved by love. You can go wild in the joy of being intoxicated by the Spirit. In other words, by singing the song of triumph you become God-intoxicated and fired with Divine enthusiasm, thereby expressing more and more of Divine love and joy every day.

You sing the song of God, or the mood of triumph, when you subjectively feel that you are that which your five senses tell you you are not; you are then God-intoxicated and seized with a Divine frenzy—a sort of mad joy.

Haven't you at times seen a person bubbling over with enthusiasm and apparently intoxicated with joy? That person was singing the Song of God at that moment. *In thy presence is fulness of joy; at thy right hand there are pleasures for evermore* (Psalm 16:11).

When you give voice to a song, you are expressing your whole nature. Your mind and body enter into the song. When your heart is full of love and goodwill, and you are radiating peace, you are truly singing God's Song; it is the song of the jubilant soul.

The real You is a spiritual, eternal, perfect being. You are a living expression of God now. *I have said, Ye are gods; and all of you are children of the most High* (Psalm 82:6).

When you pray, it is a romance with God or your Good. Your desire, when realized, brings you joy and peace. In order to realize the desire of your heart, which is depicted in The Song of Solomon as your beloved, you must woo it; let that desire of yours captivate, hold, and thrill you. Let it fire your imagination. You will always move in the direction of the desire which dominates your mind.

The majority of students of Divine Science know that The Song of Solomon is a beautiful description of the harmonious union of the conscious and subconscious mind (Solomon and Sheba).

"Tell me, O thou whom my soul loveth, where thou feedest." Your realized desire is he whom your soul loveth. You are asked "where thou feedest." In other words, what are you mentally dwelling upon? The *flock* represents your thoughts, ideas, opinions, and beliefs. You are to feast on nothing but the joy of the answered prayer.

If you are saying to yourself, "I can't. It is too late now. I am too old, and I don't know the right people"—in other words, if you are mentally feeding on all the reasons why you cannot do something or be what you want to be—you are not making "thy flock to rest at noon."

At *noon* the sun casts no shadow; likewise, when you pray, you are not to permit any shadow of fear or doubt to cross your path or deflect you from your goal or aim in life. The world of confusion shall be rejected and you shall mentally partake of, or meditate on, the reality of your desire.

"Behold, thou art fair, my love; behold, thou art fair; thou hast doves' eyes." The *dove* is a symbol of God's inner peace.

I once talked with an alcoholic who said, "Don't say anything about this God-stuff to me. I don't want God. I want a healing." This man was deeply resentful toward a former wife who had remarried; moreover, he was full of grudges against several other people. He needed the *doves' eyes*, which means he needed to see the truth that would give him peace of mind.

I asked him, "Will you pray with me now? All I ask is that you be sincere; if you are, you will experience an inner peace which passeth all human understanding."

He then relaxed his body, and I said to him, "Imagine you are talking to the Invisible Presence within you—the Almighty Power which created the Cosmos. It can do all things. Say,

'Thank you, thank you, for this inner peace.' Say it over and over again.''

After ten minutes in silent meditation, he was blinded by an interior, Inner Light. It seemed to come from the floor near where he was. The whole room was flooded with Light!

He exclaimed, ''All I see is Light! What's wrong?'' Then he relaxed into sleep in my office, and his face seemed illumined. He awakened in about fifteen minutes and was completely at peace, saying, ''God truly is! God is!'' This man had found his beloved, i.e. his sense of oneness with God and all things Good.

As you fall asleep at night, tell your desire how fair it is and how wonderful you would feel in realizing it. Begin to fall in love with your ideal. Praise it; exalt it. ''Arise, my Love!'' Feel that you are what you want to be. Go to sleep in the consciousness of being or doing what you long to do.

I once told a man on one of the islands where I was visiting to ''sleep'' on the idea of success. He was selling magazine subscriptions. He became a great success by following this procedure: I suggested that he think of success prior to sleep, i.e. what success meant to him; what he would do if he were successful. I told him to use his imagination; then, as he was about to go to sleep, to fall in love with the idea of success in this way: Repeat the one word ''success'' over and over again. He should get into the mood of success; then drop off to sleep in the arms of his Everlasting Lover, i.e. his Divine Presence, which would bring to pass whatever he accepted as true. The conditions, experiences, and events of your life are called children of your mind.

''He brought me to the banqueting house, and his banner over me was love.'' The *banquet house* is your own mind where you entertain the idea or desire of your heart.

I will illustrate at this point how to entertain in this *banquet house* of your own mind. A young girl with a special talent for singing was having great difficulty getting anything to do in the motion picture field, television, or radio. She had been turned down so often she feared she was getting a rejection complex. However, she heard me state over one of our radio programs that whatever the mind of man could imagine and feel as true, he could realize. She wrote that down, came to one of our classes, and began to practice entering into the *banquet house* by quieting the wheels of her mind and relaxing the body by simply talking to it and telling it to relax; it has to obey you. In that quiet, relaxed, peaceful state, with her attention completely focused on an imaginary movie contract in her hand, she felt the reality of the joy and wonder of it all. She was now in the *banquet house*, and the *banner* over her was *love*. *Love* is an emotional attachment. She was definitely mentally attached to this contract . . . *and calleth those things which be not as though they were* (Romans 4:17). The visible world comes out of the invisible. She caused the contract to become a reality by becoming emotionally attached to the imaginary picture of a contract in her mental *banquet house*. She knew that what she imagined and believed to be so must come to pass in the three-dimensional world.

"His left hand is under my head, and his right hand doth embrace me." The *left hand* is your deep, subjective feeling; the *right hand* is your disciplined imagination. As you begin to imagine and feel the reality of your desire, you are joining the right and left hands together in a Divine embrace; then a union of the idea and feeling takes place. Another way of saying this is: There is an agreement of the conscious and subconscious mind which denotes the answered prayer.

You know that when there is no longer any argument or doubt in your conscious or subconscious mind, your prayer is answered, because the two have agreed as touching upon it, and it is so.

"My beloved spake, and said unto me, Rise up, my love, my fair one, and come away." Is not that what your goal, aim, ambition, or desire is saying to you? For instance, the idea of perfect health is now beckoning to you and saying, "Rise up and come away from the belief in sickness, limitation, pain, and aches to health, harmony, and peace of mind."

I had a long talk with a man in England who had trouble with his leg. He had been confined to his home for nine months and was unable to lean on his leg or walk. The first thing I did was to ask him what he would do if he were healed. He said, "I would again play polo, swim, golf, and climb the Alps, which I used to do every year." That was the answer I was seeking.

I told him in the simplest way how to achieve the perfect use of his legs again. The first thing was to imagine he was actually doing the things he would do. I painted an imaginary picture for him. For fifteen or twenty minutes, three times each day, he sat in his study and imagined he was playing polo; he assumed the mental mood of actually performing the role of a polo player. He became the actor; an actor participates in the role.

Note carefully that he did not see himself playing polo; that would be an illusion. He *felt* himself playing polo. He actualized it by living the drama in his mind or *banquet house*.

At noon he would quiet the mind, still the body, and feel his Alpine clothes on him. He would feel and imagine he was climbing the Alps; he would feel the cold air on his face and hear the voices of his old associates. He lived the drama and felt the naturalness and the tangibility of the rocks.

At night prior to sleep, before going into the Arms of his Beloved—His Deeper Self—he would play a game of golf. He would hold the club, touch the ball with his hand, put it in place, and tee off. He would swing his clubs and delight in watching where the ball went. When he was in the mood of playing a good game, he would relax in a deep and healthful sleep, feeling very satisfied and happy about his experience.

Within two months this man's leg was healed, and he did all the things he imagined he would do. The *idea* of climbing the

Alps, plus the *desire* to play polo again, meant to this man, "Arise, my love, my fair one, and come away" from your belief in a physical handicap. That is what he did.

The law of the subconscious is one of compulsion. When you subjectively feel you are swimming—for example, when you feel the chill of the water and the naturalness of your various swimming strokes—you will sooner or later be compelled to swim. Whatever the handicap, whether fear or a physical condition, you will do what you subjectively felt you were doing.

Your desire, dream, ambition, goal, or aim is your saviour! It is walking down the corridor of your mind, saying to you, "Arise, my love, and come away" and enjoy the good and glorious things of life.

No matter what the problem is or its magnitude, you have really nothing to do but convince yourself of the truth which you are affirming. As quickly as you succeed in convincing yourself of the reality of your desire, results will automatically follow. Your subconscious mind will faithfully reproduce what you impregnated it with.

The Bible says, *Choose you this day whom ye will serve* (Joshua 24:15). You have the freedom to choose the tone, feeling, or mood you enter into. The manifestation of your feeling or conviction is the secret of your lover or subconscious mind. Your external actions are, therefore, determined by your subconscious beliefs and impressions.

Your thought and feeling determine your destiny. The knowledge of the truth is saying to you now, "The winter is past, the rain is over and gone." The *winter* represents that cold state when the seeds are frozen in the bosom of the earth and nothing is growing. The winter and all the seasons are in your mind.

Are your desires, dreams, visions, and aims in life frozen within you because of fear, worry, or false beliefs? You can resurrect them now by turning away from appearances, and enter into the *banquet house* of God within you, saying to yourself, "I can be what I want to be. All I have to do is to impress my subconscious mind with my desire for health, wealth, companionship, or true place, and it will express that state with which I have impressed it."

The *winter* is now over for you; the *rain* is gone, also. Your mind may have been flooded with negative thoughts, causing the mood of despondency, dejection, and melancholia. This is what a flood or avalanche of negative thoughts, false beliefs, and erroneous opinions will do. Now you know that all you have to do is to fill your mind with the truths of God which have come down to you from time immemorial. As you do this, you will crowd out of your mind everything unlike them.

The winter and the floods are over for you when regularly and systematically you fill your mind with the concepts of peace, happiness, love, and goodwill. You can do this by reading one of the Psalms, such as the Twenty-third or the Ninety-first, feeling the truth of everything you say; or you can read aloud a good meditation of the real truths of God.* As you do this, these truths go in through the eye and the ear; they release a tremendous, therapeutic vibration which courses through your entire mind and body. These curative, healing, soothing vibrations destroy, neutralize, and obliterate all the negative, fearful, diseased thoughts which caused all the trouble in your life; their embodiment must then disappear. This is prayer; do it often enough until it becomes a habit. Prayer should be a habit.

Do everything from the standpoint of the One God and His Love. For instance, when you shop, pray before purchasing. Say, "God guides me in all my purchases." Say quietly to the saleslady or salesman, "God is prospering you."

---

*See, for example, the author's *Special Meditations for Health, Wealth, Love, and Expression* and *Quiet Moments with God*, both published by DeVorss & Company.

Whatever you do, do it with love and goodwill. Pour out love, peace, and goodwill to all. Claim frequently that God's Love and Transcendent Beauty flow through all your thoughts, words, and actions. Make a habit of this. Fill your mind with the eternal verities; then you will see that "The flowers appear on the earth; the time of the singing of birds is come"! You begin to *flower*; yes, you will begin to blossom forth.

The *earth* means your body, environment, social life, and all things necessary on this objective plane.

The *flowers* you witness will be the birth of God in your mind. The *flowers* of God's Guidance will watch over you and lead you to green pastures and still waters. The flowers of God's Love will fill your heart. Now, instead of seeing discord anywhere, you will see the Love of God operating in all His Creation; as you realize It, you will see love come forth and flower in the other.

When you go into a home and you see confusion, quarrelling, and strife, you will realize within yourself that the peace of God reigns supreme in the minds and hearts of all those in this house; you will see the flower of peace made manifest and expressed.

When you see financial lack and limitation, you will realize the infinite abundance and wealth of God forever flowing, filling up all the empty vessels and leaving a Divine surplus. As you do this, you will live in the garden of God where only orchids and similar flowers of great beauty grow; for only God's ideas circulate in your mind.

As you go to sleep every night, you will clothe yourself with the garment of love, peace, and joy. From now on you always go to sleep feeling that you now are what you long to be. Your last concept as you fall asleep is etched on your deeper mind; you shall resurrect it. Always take into the *banquet house* of your lover (subconscious mind) a noble, God-like concept of yourself; your lover (subconscious mind) will always give you what you conceive and believe as true. Anything you can conceive, you can achieve. Love gives birth to all things. Your tomorrows are determined by your concept of yourself as you fall asleep in the arms of your lover (your ideal).

The time of the singing of birds is at hand for you when you cease singing that old song of lack. You have listened to people sing this kind of song; it is like an old phonograph record: "I'm so lonesome; things never went right for me. I never had a chance. I have been cruelly treated." "I have been operated on three times." "You should hear about all the money I lost." Yes, then they tell about the fear on the lonely road, plus their likes, dislikes, pet peeves, and hates. Imbued with God's love, you will no longer sing that song again. You will sing the new song; for God's ideas and truths (*birds*) will sing in you.

Then you will speak in a new tongue, which means the mood of peace, joy, goodwill, and love. You will no longer react to people and conditions as you formerly did. The Song of God is now heard. Now when someone says something mean or nasty to you, you will immediately transform it by realizing that God's peace fills your soul. You will consume it with the fire of right thoughts; the birds will truly sing in your mind and heart as you do. You are happy; you are bubbling over with enthusiasm, and you are looking forward with a joyous expectancy to all good things. Wherever you go, you carry peace with you; all those who come within your orbit are blessed by your inner radiance. You begin to see sermons in stones, tongues in trees, songs in running brooks, and God in everything. *The voice of the turtledove* is now heard in your land!

Tennyson said, "Speak to Him thou, for He hears, spirit with spirit shall meet, closer is He than breathing, and nearer than hands and feet."

The voice of the turtledove is the voice of peace, the voice of intuition and of God's inner Guidance. You can hear it by lowly listening. For instance, one time as a boy I was lost in the woods. I sat down under a tree and remembered a prayer which starts with, "Our Father, He will show us the way; let us be quiet, and He will lead us." I quietly repeated, "Father, lead us."

A wave of peace came over me which I can still recall. *The voice of the turtledove* became real. The *turtledove* is intuition, which means being taught from within. An overpowering feeling came over me to go in a certain direction as if I were being pushed ahead. Two of the boys came with me; the others did not. We were led out of that thick jungle as if by an Unseen Hand.

Great musicians have listened and heard the music within; they wrote down what they heard inwardly. In meditation Lincoln listened to the principle of liberty; Beethoven heard the principle of harmony.

If you are intensely interested in the science of mathematics, you are loving it; as you love it, it will reveal all its secrets to you.

Jesus heard *the voice of the turtledove* when he said, *Peace I leave with you; my peace I give unto you; not as the world giveth, give I unto you. Let not your heart be troubled; neither let it be afraid* (John 14:27). How wonderful you will feel as you drink in these words and fill your mind with their therapeutic potency!

Job heard *the voice of the turtledove* when he said, *Acquaint now thyself with Him, and be at peace* (Job 22:21). *Thou wilt keep him in perfect peace, whose mind is stayed on thee: because he trusteth in thee* (Isaiah 26:3). *For God is not the author of confusion, but of peace* (1 Corinthians 14:33).

You can hear *the voice of the turtledove* by turning to the Infinite Intelligence within you, saying, "Father, this is what I want . . . "; then state specifically and clearly the thing you desire. You are now turning your desire over to the God-Wisdom within you, which knows all, sees all, and has the "know-how" of accomplishment. You always know whether you have really turned your request over or not. If you are at peace about it, you have turned it over. If you are anxious and worried, you have not subjectified your prayer; you do not fully trust the God-Wisdom within.

If you want guidance, claim that Infinite Intelligence is guiding you now; It will differentiate Itself as right action for you. You will know you have received the answer, for the dove of peace will whisper in your ear, "Peace, be still." You will know the Divine answer, for you will be at peace, and your decision will be right.

A girl was wondering recently whether to accept a position in New York for considerably more money or remain in Los Angeles in her present position. At night as she went to sleep, she asked herself this question: "What would be my reaction if I had made the right decision now?" The answer came to her, "I would feel wonderful. I would feel happy having made the right decision," and she began to say, "Isn't it wonderful! Isn't it wonderful!" over and over again, as a lullaby, and lulled herself to sleep in the feeling, "It is wonderful."

She had a dream that night, and the voice in the dream said, "Stand still! Stand still!" She awakened immediately and knew of course that this was *the voice of the turtledove*—the voice of intuition.

The fourth-dimensional self within her can see ahead; it knows all and sees all; it can read the minds of the owners of the business in New York. She remained in her present position. Subsequent events proved the truth of her Inner Voice; the eastern concern went into bankruptcy. *I the Lord will make myself known unto him in a vision, and will speak unto him in a dream* (Numbers 12:6).

"My beloved is mine, and I am his; he feedeth among the lilies." The *lilies* represent the poppies which grow in the East. To see the poppy field sway in the breeze is a very beautiful sight. Here the inspired biblical writer is telling you to have a romance with God-like qualities in your mind. As you turn to the God-Presence, It turns to you. You experience the mystic marriage, the wedded bliss, when you fall madly in love with truth for truth's sake; then you become full of the new wine, the new interpretation of life.

The *lilies* symbolize beauty, order, symmetry, and proportion. As you feed or feast on the great truth that God is Indescribable Beauty, Boundless Love, Absolute Bliss, Absolute Harmony, and Infinite Peace, you are truly *feeding among the lilies*. When you claim that what is true of God is true of you, miracles will happen in your life.

By realizing and knowing that these qualities and attributes of God are being expressed through you and that you are a channel for the Divine, every atom of your being begins to dance to the rhythm of the Eternal God. Beauty, order, harmony, and peace appear in your mind, body, and business world as you *feed among the lilies*; you feel your oneness with God, Life, and God's Infinite Riches. You are married to your Beloved, for you are now married to your ideal or desire; you are a bride of the Lord—your dominant conviction. From this moment forward you will bring forth children of your Beloved; they will bear the image and likeness of your idea and feeling.

The father is God's idea; the mother is the emotionalizing of the idea, and its subjective embodiment. From that union of idea and feeling comes forth your health, abundance, happiness, and inner peace.

Sit down and *feed among the lilies* by realizing that every night of the year when you go to sleep, you go before the King of Kings, the Lord of Lords, and the Prince of Peace. Be sure you are "dressed properly" as you enter into the Divine Presence. If you were going before the President, you would put on your best clothes. The clothes you wear as you enter into the heavens of your own mind every night represent the mood, or the tone you wear. Be sure it is always the wedding garment of love, peace, and goodwill to all.

Be absolutely sure that you can say, "Behold, thou art fair." There must be no resentment, ill-will, condemnation of self or others, and no criticism of any person. God's Love must really fill your heart for all men everywhere. You must sincerely wish for everyone what you wish for yourself; then you can say to your mood or feeling, "Behold, thou art fair." *And when ye stand praying, forgive, if ye have ought against any* (Mark 11:25).

"My beloved is mine." All that God is, is yours, for God is within you. All you can possibly desire is already yours. You need no help from the outside to *feed among the lilies.*

When you go to sleep tonight, forgive everyone, and imagine and feel that your desire is fulfilled. Become absolutely and completely indifferent to all thought of failure, because you now know the law. As you accept the end, you have, as Troward so beautifully stated, "willed the means to the realization of the end." As you are about to enter sleep, galvanize yourself into the feeling of being or having your desire. Your mental acceptance of your desire as you go to sleep is your oneness with your Beloved; then this is your conviction in the subconscious mind which gives you that which you impressed upon it.

He feedeth among the lilies. Until the day break, and the shadows flee away. The *shadows* are fear, doubt, worry, anxiety, and all the reasons why you cannot do something. The *shadows* of our five senses and the race belief hover over the minds of all as we pray.

When you pray, accept as true what your reason and five senses deny and reject. Remain faithful to your idea by being full of faith every step of the way. When your consciousness is fully qualified with the acceptance of your desire, all the fear will go away. Trust in the reality of your ideal or desire until you are filled full of the feeling of being it; then you will experience the joy of the answered prayer. Yes, the answer to your prayer will come and light up the heavens of your mind, bringing you peace.

No matter what the problem is, nor how acute, dark, or hopeless things seem to be, turn now to God and say, "How is it in God and Heaven?" The answer will softly steal over your mind like the dew from heaven: "All is peace, joy, bliss, perfection, wholeness, harmony, and beauty." Then reject the evidence of your senses, and *feed among the lilies* of God and Heaven, such as peace, harmony, joy, and perfection. Realize that what is true of God also must be true of you and your surroundings. Continue in this abiding trust and faith in God *until the day break and the shadows flee away.*